THERE WAS ONLY ONE PERFECT MAN WHO EVER LIVED

THE REST OF US HAVE TO SWIM

GUY PARRISH

THERE WAS ONLY ONE PERFECT MAN WHO EVER LIVED: THE REST OF US HAVE TO SWIM

PROMINENT
BOOKS
EDGE

5830 E 2nd St, Ste 7000 #9983
Casper, WY 82609
USA

ACKNOWLEDGEMENTS

No book or even task on this earth is a one-man endeavor. It is with my most sincere thanks to God that He has sent a lot of wonderful people into my life. This book would still be in the planning stage if it weren't for some of them.

To my Lord and Savior Jesus Christ—Thank you Lord for Grace it is so amazing! Without your grace there would have never been a book, and even worse than that there wouldn't be a life that I call "my life." My life would be caught up in a web of sin without hope. You came to me when I was 16 and I will never, be the same again. You can walk on water and I am so glad you can!

To Keleta my faithful wife—Sweetheart you are literally one in a million and you are the sunshine of my life. Without you my inspiration to write would be limited. God gave me grace by giving me you. You are three times a lady and I love you!

To Teresa Riddle—Words could never really say how much your help in completing this project has meant to me. You without a doubt have been the best assistant I have ever had. Thanks for the countless hours you have spent in front of the computer correcting, proofing, proofing again, correcting again, taking out words, adding words, typing, typing and more typing to make this dream a reality. Your tireless enthusiasm over this book will never be forgotten.

To Clifford Hurst—Thanks for the selfless hours you poured into this project. Your discerning eye, wise counsel and accuracy have helped me beyond description. And to think it was all for nothing (that is no money). Your expertise is invaluable and your friendship in priceless.

To Betty Gore—Thank you so very much for your keen awareness and impeccable literary skill. I know you weren't feeling well when you proofed the manuscript so it goes without saying, your dedication is to be commended. May the Lord bless you.

To Gene Speck—Thanks again for all your help in the publishing of this book. I appreciate our friendship and count it a great blessing to have you and Beverly as friends.

To Rev. Leon McDowell—Bro. Mac. thank you for being my pastor. As a teen-age boy you taught me grace not just from the pulpit but also by your example. God blessed me with a great Pastor!

To Andy Middleton—Since this is my second book and since I didn't mention you in my first. Here it is so please quit griping (just a joke). Beaker we have been friends since the 5th grade and at our age that is a long time. But really thanks for all the phone calls that provoke my thinking and a life long friendship. I am so glad you know God's grace and we will have eternity to cut up and act crazy.

To Timmy Williams—What can I say Timmy; you single handedly encouraged me to finish this book more than anyone else. You are like family to me and I can honestly say when God created you He broke the mold! God's grace is believable when I see you. You are incredible!

CONTENTS

CHAPTER ONE
Casting Out the Ghost of the Past..1

CHAPTER TWO
You Can't Live Life Without An Eraser...11

CHAPTER THREE
Retroactive Righteousness 23

CHAPTER FOUR
Super Sinners Need Super Grace 32

CHAPTER FIVE
The Humpty Dumpty Dilemma..42

CHAPTER SIX
Who Was That Masked Man?..53

CHAPTER SEVEN
Mercy Draped in Skin 63

CHAPTER EIGHT
The Color of Redemption 72

CHAPTER NINE
From the Mire to the Choir..82

CHAPTER TEN
Have You Heard Any Good News Lately? 91

CHAPTER ELEVEN
On a Clear Day You Can See Forever...108

CHAPTER TWELVE
He Did Walk On Water 121

This book
is lovingly and affectionately dedicated
to my only daughter,

Shanta LaFaithe.

You are grace in the flesh and your life
is an inspiration to me.
You are my little "Snows Elsie"
as well as daddy's girl.
I am so blessed by having you.
I love you so much!

CHAPTER ONE

CASTING OUT THE GHOST OF THE PAST

━━━◆◆◆◆◆◆◆━━━

IT WAS ONE of those dark nights; you know, the kind you see in an Alfred Hitchcock classic thriller. The trees softly shook as a gentle breeze blew by. The moon and all the stars were obscured from sight by a low-hanging ceiling of thick slate-colored clouds. My wife and I were in the little sleepy town of Eureka Springs, Arkansas. It was almost midnight, so for the fun of it, we went to the Crescent Hotel, which is not any ordinary hotel. The Crescent Moon is over one hundred years old and has a long and lustrous history. Within its walls have occurred a famous and celebrated sensation the documented, so-called ghost sightings.

After leaving the observation deck we came down a long spiraling staircase and found ourselves in line with a small group of people. I thought this was rather strange considering the lateness of the hour, so I asked a young man what this was all about. He said, "We are taking a ghost tour," and then he added, "We are not going for another fifteen minutes, so you still have time to get your tickets." Did we go? No! Do we believe in ghosts? No! Did we stay in the hotel for the night? No! Besides, the hot tub wasn't big enough for Guy, Keleta, and Casper!

Now, before you jump to conclusions, let me state for the record that I do not in any way believe in ghosts and goblins. Emphatically and absolutely not! I believe like the gifted English poet George Herbert, who said, "If you see a ghost at night, the thing to do is, go up and speak to it, and you will find the ghost is nothing more than a sheet hung out to dry!" The ghosts of human beings that once lived just simply do not exist on this earth. Haunted houses are only the figment of men's dark imaginations. However, I will tell you what is not illusionary, in the case of multitudes of people, the house of their soul is haunted by some ghost of their past: A sin committed or an evil deed done; an illicit lifestyle or a bad influence on a son or daughter. Your mind is like a VCR, and you keep hitting the rewind and play, rewind and play. The past is like a fabled vampire that sucks out all the joy of living and murders sleep.

Oh, that it were possible thus to undo the past! "I would give my life," said John B. Gough, "If I could undo the things this guilty hand has done!" In the haunted and tormented minds of many the answer comes resounding back, "Impossible, it cannot be!" But, the truth that sets men free still stands like a tenfold beacon in the night: "If we confess our sins, he is faithful and just to forgive us our sins, and to cleanse us from all unrighteousness" (1 John 1:9). "And their sins and iniquities will I remember no more" (Hebrews 10:17). Divine mercy and eternal grace have been forever given that the past may be blotted out, and the hope of a new life now stands as an ever-present possibility before us. The pain of yesterday may be submerged in the depths of the unfathomable sea of God's grace, never to be seen again. What was otherwise impossible is now made possible through the power of God's grace.

Horatio Gates Spafford articulated this truth with a masterful stroke when he penned the words to that old church hymn, "It is Well with My Soul":

"My sin, oh the bliss of this glorious tho't:

My sin, not in part, but the whole,

Is nailed to the cross and I bear it no more,

Praise the Lord, praise the Lord, O my soul!"

What a wonderful God!

There's a story of a preacher in the Philippines, a much loved man of God, who carried the burden of a secret sin he had committed many years before. He had repented but still had no peace, no sense of God's forgiveness. When anything bad or any misfortune would occur in his life, he would instantly feel it was God's punishment for his former sin. In his church was a woman who deeply loved God and who claimed to have visions in which she spoke with Christ and He with her. The preacher, however, was skeptical. To test her he said, "The next time you speak with Christ, I want you to ask him what sin your pastor committed while he was in seminary." The woman agreed. A few days later the pastor asked, "Well, did Christ visit you in your dreams?"

"Yes, he did," she replied.

"And did you ask him what sin I committed in seminary?"

"Yes."

"Well, what did he say?"

"He said, 'I don't remember…'"

What God forgives, he forgets!

The night Jesus was betrayed was possibly the darkest night of human history. The wheels of redemption stood still while the Son of God wrestled with an invisible cup. In the agony of His soul, He cried out in the garden of Gethsemane, "Father, if it be possible let this cup pass from me, but nevertheless, not my will but thy will be done!" The struggle was ended, and He drank the cup. He rose up and returned to His disciples, whom He found in a stupor of sleep. In moments they were awakened by a multitude led by Judas.

Jesus was now surrounded by a delegation from the high Priest's court and threatened by the armed Roman soldiers. Unexpectedly, Peter lunged out of the shadow and shouted, "Shall we smite them with the sword, Lord?" Then, there was the lantern light flickering off a blade and suddenly it was over someone's head. Out of the darkness came a cry of agony from Malchus, the high priest's servant, "Ah…!" He was holding the side of his face as with every pump of his heart the hot blood gushed out of the side of his head.

Before this night the religious leaders who hated Jesus could only falsely accuse Him. Now there is a charge to be made. Now violence can be attributed to Jesus. Now we see they are revolutionaries. Now we see the disciples are like the other men in prison for starting factions and revolting against the Caesar. See, they have used the sword; they have stricken and cut off the ear of the servant to the great high priest! Now, their enemies have the evidence!

Everyone is in trouble now, especially the disciple who did that impulsive and irrational act of violence. Peter was in a big predicament. It was an open and shut case that even O.J. Simpson's lawyers wouldn't have been able to get him out of. A thousand Philadelphia lawyers would have been helpless in getting an acquittal. He was guilty, caught in the act, caught on tape.

The multitude, the Roman soldiers, Judas, the high priest, and the other ten disciples were all eyewitnesses. Even Jesus, who could never lie, would be brought in as a key witness for He was only five feet from where the crime was committed. Peter's fingerprints were on the sword and, Malchus's blood was splashed all over Peter's body. The ear of Malchus lay severed on the ground and thus could become Exhibit #1. Peter was dead in the water, in a manner of speaking.

But Jesus did something that no one was expecting. He reached out His hand, picked up the ear, compassionately laid it on the side of the high priest servant's head, and healed him!

THERE WAS ONLY ONE PERFECT MAN WHO EVER LIVED THE REST OF US HAVE TO SWIM

The crime was committed and because Peter was a preacher and even one of the twelve, he was not above the law. No one is. He may have wished, after he committed the crime, that he hadn't, but it was too late. He would have to live with that ghost the rest of his life, which probably wasn't very long. Peter was just seconds away from being arrested, tried, sentenced, and crucified for his crime. But, faster than the speed of light, Jesus through the power of grace justified this disciple by destroying all evidence of the crime.

Peter couldn't be accused of anything now because the ear was back on. There was no cut, bruise, or even a scar. Malchus was now holding the side of his face screaming, "I'm all right! I'm all right! I'm healed!" It would be foolish to bring a man to trial without any evidence.

Justification has been described in these terms, "Just as if we had never sinned." Jesus in a real way justified Peter that chaotic night in the garden. For He in one swift and sure move took away the evidence against Peter by healing Malchus. He took away the guilt by taking away the crime.

There have been many imaginative methods employed to destroy and dispose of evidence. The criminal mastermind has in many cases escaped conviction by simply causing the evidence to disappear. Murder weapons have been disassembled and thrown to the four winds. Eye-witnesses have been murdered. Fingerprints have been wiped clean, and judges and whole juries have been threatened or paid off. But, Jesus took away the evidence by a miracle!

You and I are just as guilty as Peter for crimes and sins we have committed. We crucified the Lord of Glory. There we stood with His blood dripping from our hands, still holding the whip and hammer. Supernatural forensic science has found our DNA at the crime scene. Our fingerprints are on the nails, the hammer, and the cross, where we lifted Him up between heaven and earth. Nature, sin, the past, and all of heaven stand ready to testify against us. We killed Him and are as guilty as sin.

Here is the miracle: We crucified the Lord, but it is that crucifixion that justified us and set us free! You have a sin? He has a solution. You have a past? He has a pardon. You have a debt? He has deliverance!

"Wait just a minute," you might say. "What would Jesus say about adultery?" He would say, "Neither do I condemn you, go and sin no more." Well, what of murder, lying or embezzlement? The answer is simple: "Forgiven!" Maybe you have been told, "You've made your bed, now sleep in it." But that is not what Jesus said. He told the man sick with the palsy who was let down through the roof by his four friends, "Take up thy bed and walk, your sins are forgiven!" That is what He says to every poor soul that struggles with the past, if that soul would only confess and believe.

Now understand this: we haven't been acquitted; we've been justified, and there is a difference. If one is "acquitted", that means there is insufficient or not enough evidence to bring a conviction. The authorities are going to drop the charges and kick the case out of court.

Such acquittal is like the case of old Willie, who was brought into court with the charge of stealing chickens from his neighbor. After the case was presented, the judge had no other option but to drop the charges and acquit Willie because of the lack of evidence. The judge brought down his wooden gavel and said, "Well, Willie, I guess I have no other choice but to acquit you for stealing chickens." To that Willie replied, "Do that mean I've got to take them chickens back, judge?"

We have been eternally justified and not acquitted in the sight of the Great Judge. Being justified, we are as though we never committed the act of disobedience. Only God can clear the record and wipe the slate clean. Thank God, He can!

In the fall of 1983 I had just re-enrolled as a junior in college. One afternoon the school office was approached by one of the local farmers. He was in dire need of a little help and was willing to pay a fair wage. I was a full time student, so money was as scarce as pork in pork &

beans. When the announcement was made, I never hesitated a minute in signing up. Four of us went to work for the old farmer. When we arrived at the farm, he began to give us our chores, and I got the job of driving the tractor. It was time to sow the winter wheat. My grandpa George Koelsch was a farmer, and I grew up riding "Old Allie," the orange, 1953 model Allis-Chalmers. Yet, I had never actually driven one all by myself. But I caught on quick, and in no time I was plowing furrows and planting seed. For hours I turned that good ol' Missouri soil and sowed winter wheat. When "dark-thirty" finally came (that's a farmer's term for thirty minutes after dark), I looked as though God had just created me right out of the soil. There was dirt in my hair, in my teeth, on my face, and on my hands. There was dirt in my shoes. When I took my clothes off, the dirt and dust had sifted through, and I looked like the creature from the dirt lagoon. But, then I stepped into the shower and washed ever so clean. When I reemerged, there was not one trace of evidence that I had ever been in the field. All the evidence had washed down the drain, and it was gone. That is a picture of what justification, grace, and forgiveness can do to sin. The blood of Jesus Christ cleanses us from all unrighteousness! Under the flow of His blood all the evidence is washed away! This truth is expressed in the song that William Cowper wrote so many years ago, "There is a Fountain Filled with Blood"' Inspirationally and poignantly he penned these life- changing words in the first verse,

> There is a fountain filled with blood,
> Drawn from Immanuel's veins,
> And sinners plunged beneath that flood,
> Lose all their guilty stains.

"When Pilate saw that he could prevail nothing, but that rather a tumult was made, he took water, and washed his hands before the multitude, saying, I am innocent of the blood of this just person: see ye to it," (Matthew 27:24).

Legend has it that after Pilate made his decision to give the people Jesus and release Barabbas, he was haunted by his actions for the rest of his life. His decision became a phobia with him that he could not escape. He washed his hands every few minutes but could never wash away the guilt of shedding the innocent blood of Jesus. A little water could easily wash that off the actual blood. But, was there something beneath bloodguilt?

In truth, the trouble lay deeper down; it was the ingrained sense of sin. Again, there is irony! The innocent blood he shed that so haunted him was the same blood that could cleanse him, if he, like many others, would just accept it. All the water in all the oceans, ponds, and lakes can never wash away the act of sin or the guilt of the past; but, one drop of Christ's blood can totally annihilate any evidence of past sin, and that person through a miracle can become a new creation.

In the Civil War during the Campaign in the Wilderness, the Confederate officers were tipped off that spies were to be sent through the lines to find out the disposition of their troops. A number of sharp-shooters were put on sentinel detail and given the order to shoot on sight and ask questions later. One certain sniper was positioned on a hillside that overlooked an orchard with thick woods beyond. At dusk three suspicious men made their way through the woods and entered the orchard. The moment became intense as the sniper lowered his musket and took aim at one of the men dodging from tree to tree.

Though he had been in many battles, he had consciously never taken aim at one particular person and instantly terminated his life. That thought sent a chill down his spine. He had mortal dread of sending a soul into eternity; therefore, he could not pull the trigger. However, a sense of ethical duty overcame him, and he lowered his weapon again; and, this time, carrying out his order, he fired. The Union spy threw up his hands and with a gush of blood from his forehead fell with his hands outstretched. His two comrades turned and ran back into the thick of the woods.

That night the sharpshooter could not rest. The vivid picture of the dead man was burned onto his retina. The image assassinated his sleep! As time passed, the war ended but the image of the dead man in the orchard was ever before him. It was as if the ghost of the dead man had attached itself to the sniper's tranquility, joy and peace. He fell into a deep melancholy, which he could never shake.

Many years after the Great War between the states he boarded a train. As he sat, he noticed the man directly in front wore an ex-military badge on the lapel of his coat. It was evident he was an ex-Union soldier. They struck up conversation, which naturally led to reminiscences of the war. In the course of conversation the Union soldier told the graphic epic of his narrow escape while serving in the Wilderness Campaign.

He had been dispatched with two other soldiers to infiltrate Confederate ranks and discover the strategic position of the enemy. They had just left a wooded area and entered into an orchard where he must have given into carelessness, for a musket ball struck him dead center of his forehead. He immediately lost all consciousness of the world around him.

His companions fled, but under the cover of darkness they returned and carried him to a field hospital where he lay for weeks in a delirium. Then he said, "My recovery was a miracle!" He raised his hat and showed the Confederate soldier the scar in the center of his forehead and the scar in back of his head where the musket ball had plowed through and made an exit. Up until this point the ex-sniper had listened in silence with his heart in his throat. But now, he sprang to his feet and screamed for joy! The horror of all those tormented years was gone! The ghost of the past was cast out. He was justified by a miracle and set free in an instant. It was as though it never happened!

In Isaiah 38:17, the prophet writes of his full pardon:

Behold, for peace I had great bitterness: but thou hast in love to my soul delivered it from the pit of corruption: for thou hast cast all my sins behind thy back.

I have but one question: If God has put your sin behind, then why don't you?

CHAPTER TWO

YOU CAN'T LIVE LIFE WITHOUT AN ERASER

❦

I HAD A dream that I had died and gone to heaven, and, as I was preparing to enter into New Jerusalem, the heavenly city, I was met at the gate by a very large angel. The angel had something golden in his hand. As I walked closer to him, he put out his hand. It was a golden holder. I opened it, and it was a piece of chalk. The angel said, "You have made it to heaven, but it's very important to know and realize how great a salvation you have. I want you to take this piece of chalk, right over here, and I want you to write down all the sins you ever committed and have been forgiven of."

As I turned to walk away, I noticed that the clouds opened up, and there was a big red ladder. And, as I walked toward the ladder with the piece of chalk in my hand and began to write all these sins, I thought, there's no way I can ever remember all the sins I ever committed.

But the funniest thing happened: Suddenly, I began to remember the earliest days of my being a human being. And then I remembered all the sins I committed, even as a child. I began to write down on each rung of the ladder the various different sins I had committed in my lifetime. I had an uncanny ability to remember every day of my life.

As I wrote those sins down and kept writing, I didn't realize how high I had gotten up on the ladder. The ground was story after story after story below me. And I wrote and wrote and wrote, and pretty soon the ground was but a distant memory. It was hard to see.

I ran out of chalk; so, I had to climb all the way back down the ladder. I went down the ladder all the way back to the ground, and I went and found the angel. I must admit I was really embarrassed. I said, "I'm humiliated to say, but I need more chalk." He said, "That sometimes happens."

So he handed me another piece of chalk, and I went back over to the ladder. I climbed and climbed and climbed all the way back to the top and began writing again and again and again. Finally, after a long time, I was near the end of my sins. I could even remember the very sins I'd committed the day before I died, so I knew I was getting close to the end.

I was about to write the last sin on the last rung of the ladder. I had reduced the chalk down to a tiny little piece. As I was about to put my hand down on that rung to write the last sin, this giant foot came down from above and stepped on my hand. I looked up, and it was my younger brother Todd. He said, "Guy, do you have anymore chalk, by chance?"

I hope you recognize this as a joke that I meant to be funny. Not that I am making light of sin but am trying to drive home the reality that, as long as we are in a mortal body, sin is a possibility or rather a probability. It is inevitable, and I doubt that anyone who would argue the fact would tell the truth about anything. Believe it or not, I do remember one of the first sins I committed. And, ironically, it revolves around an eraser. Not just any eraser, but an unbelievable, big, green rubber eraser! I was in the first grade when a girl in my class brought this incredible eraser to school. It was the biggest eraser I had ever seen, and green was and still is my favorite color. The little sinful man down inside of me said, "I want that eraser, and I am going to get it!" I was captivated and almost put into a spell. So in my little devious six-year-old mind, I developed a plan: When recess was called and everyone was outside on the playground, I snuck back into the classroom, went to her chair and opened her desk. There it was: It was glorious, stupendous, breathtaking, stunning, and now it was mine. I quickly stuffed it in my jeans and ran back outside. All that day I watched the clock and could hardly wait until I could get home and examine my ill-gotten treasure. Finally the clock struck the last minute of school, and I hurriedly grabbed my stuff and headed for the bus. On the bus, I felt so good that I had pulled off the heist of my short lifetime. I was a first grade, petty extortionist, plain and simple. Once I was at home I went to my room and pulled my prized loot from my jeans. It was everything I knew it would be. You would have thought I had stolen the Hope Diamond. I was clear; no one had seen me, and no one could catch me now. Wrong! God not only saw me, but God had a way of catching me too.

To this day I cannot explain the events that followed. My big, green, rubber eraser was hidden deep in my room when my dad came home from work. For some bizarre reason he had to go to the same little girl's house that I had stolen the eraser from, and he told me to go with him. I don't remember how my dad and her dad even knew each other and why he suddenly had to go to their home. I immediately knew I was busted, but how? I remember praying to God and bargaining. I basically told Him, if He would work a miracle and somehow get me out of this dreadful bind I had put myself in, that tomorrow, I promised, I would take the eraser back and I would never do it again.

Reluctantly, I went with my dad, and it seemed we were there for eternity doing whatever he was doing there. The classmate and I were sitting in the living room. I felt sure I had been set up and that at any moment I would be interrogated. But nothing was ever brought up and I was never put under the bright lights and given the third degree. When we left, the good feeling I had on the bus after I had stolen the eraser didn't even come close to the euphoria that filled my soul. I felt God had kept His end of the bargain and somehow worked the miraculous.

So I kept my end of the bargain and the next day I snuck back into classroom during recess and put the big green eraser back in her desk. But, you know, it didn't seem quite as big that day. I learned a lifetime lesson I will never forget: Be sure God sees you and you cannot cover your sin. "He that covereth his sins shall not prosper: but whoso confesseth and forsaketh [them] shall have mercy," (Proverbs 28:13). Only the blood of Jesus can cover sin!

Whether we want to admit it or not, life is filled with mistakes, shortcomings, and sins. Thank God for the power of a good eraser! God has one; oh, you didn't read Psalms 103:12? "As far as the east is from the west, [so] far hath he removed our transgressions from us." That is to say you can go east as far as you want to go, and you will never run into the west. When God erases your sin, you will never run into those sins again. They will never be brought up, evaluated, nit picked or examined again. When asking Jesus about your sin, He will reply, "What sins are you talking about? I can't remember them anymore." The question has been asked, "Is there anything God can't do?" And the answer is yes! He cannot see my sins under the blood of Jesus. The old adage is "Out of sight out of mind."

If God is willing to forget your sins, don't you think you should let them go? Really you can't live life without an eraser. Paul said, "Not as though I had already attained, either were already perfect: but I follow after, if that I may apprehend that for which also I am apprehended of Christ Jesus. Brethren, I count not myself to have apprehended: but [this] one thing [I do], forgetting those things which are behind, and reaching forth unto those things which are before, I press toward the mark for the prize of the high calling of God in Christ Jesus" (Philippians 3:12–14). Paul admittedly says, if you will allow me to paraphrase, "I haven't made it yet folks. I haven't attained that state of perfection. I am still not all I should be for Jesus. I have not arrived, but I am on my way;

and I am giving all my energies to get there. It takes erasing my failures of the past and pressing forward toward a mark that is the finish line to receive the prize of heaven. By God's grace and help you can count me in I will be there one day. So don't count me out."

Mark Twain once said, "If a cat sits on a hot stove it will never sit on a hot stove again. Of course it will never sit on a cold stove either." For some people the sins and failures of the past keeps them at a complete standstill. They have lost their vision, faith, and expectancy for the future. The pressing and moving forward is reduced to an idle.

Out of literally millions of golfers very few have ever attained the success, skill, and mastery of the sport of golf like the great Arnold Palmer. You can count them on your fingers. But I read that in 1961 in the Los Angeles Open at the height of Arnold Palmer's lustrous career he took a 12 on the ninth hole. To this day at the Rancho Park Golf Course where it all took place they have erected a bronze plate that states, "On Friday January 6, 1961, the first day of the 35th Los Angeles Open, Arnold Palmer, voted Golfer of the Year and Pro Athlete of the Year, took a 12 on this hole." He was asked about that dreadful and embarrassing day and of the ninth hole. He replied, "That doggone plaque will be there long after I am gone. But you have to put things behind you. That's one of the wonderful things about golf. Your next shot can be as good or bad as your last one but you'll always get another chance." That gives every duffer in the world hope!

God has erased your every bad shot, bad thought, and bad sin off His hard drive. When will you? God's grace is one more chance! Do you think Adam and Eve only sinned once? Someone has coined the phrase, "He is the God of the second chance." I agree, but he is also the God of the chance that can't be numbered. Jesus taught us to pray for forgiveness everyday we are alive. You don't believe me? Then turn your Bible to what has been traditionally called "The Lord's Prayer." "Give us day by day our daily bread. And forgive us our sins…" (Luke 11:3–4). Oh, He has forgotten the sins of your past, but, unfortunately, you accumulate more everyday. Fortunately God has a big eraser.

There is another part of asking for forgiveness that is in the same prayer, and that is the business of erasing the sins that other have sinned against you. "And forgive us our sins; for we also forgive every one that is indebted to us" (Luke 11:4). Matthew's Gospel renders it this way, "And forgive us our debts, as we forgive our debtors" (Matthew 6:12). When someone does us wrong and we feel they have sinned against us, we feel they have become indebted to us. They owe us an apology, respect, and love again. And, bless God, we are not going to forget it, and we will hold them accountable for the debt until they humbly come get on their knees and pay us. But this attitude is not what Jesus taught.

What is forgiveness? Forgiveness is a divine action for which there is a human parallel. Through forgiveness we imitate and emulate the character of God. When we forgive we act like God. John writes to show us God's nature. "…He is faithful and just to forgive us [our] sins, and to cleanse us from all unrighteousness," (I John 1:9).

Jesus clearly commands forgiveness: "And when ye stand praying, forgive, if ye have ought against any: that your Father also which is in heaven may forgive you your trespasses. But if ye do not forgive, neither will your Father which is in heaven forgive your trespasses" (Mark 11:25–26). Forgiveness is an unmistakable obligation of the Kingdom lifestyle.

Jesus connects forgiveness to our prayer lives. If we expect God to hear and answer our prayers, then the first requirement on our part is to forgive people that have done us wrong. Not only does Jesus tie our forgiveness to the effectiveness of our prayer lives, but He also connects forgiveness to the quality of our relationship to the Father and receiving our own forgiveness from Him.

You don't have to know Greek or Hebrew to understand what Jesus is saying. You may have been able to hold on to those old unforgiving feelings you have towards someone in your past but today is the day of your awaking! After reading this, now that you know the truth, and God is even bringing witness to your spirit, if you refuse to let go of that old, hard, and unforgiving spirit, don't expect God to get in a hurry to forgive you of your sins! You've been walking around for years with unhealed, inflexible, and unforgiving spirits about legitimate hurts, things that have happened to you, that have hurt you deeply. That brings a question: Why should we forgive? Let me give you two excellent reasons:

1.   Because our Lord commands it

Forgiveness is not a suggestion or recommendation. Jesus doesn't say, "It would be a good idea that you forgive; or, I have always discovered in my life forgiveness works the best, and I offer it to you as a viable alternative in your lifestyle." He commands it—plain and simple. It is a divine command that is not optional; God's commands must be fleshed out.

2.   Because it is in your best interest to forgive

If you want your prayers answered and if you want God to forgive your sins, you must be willing to forgive others. It's only being fair to you. Everybody that reads these words has been hurt, either by people or circumstances. All of us have been let down by someone we believed we could count on. All of us have been treated like a stranger by someone we thought was an intimate friend and been betrayed by a so-called friend to whom we really gave credence. We have all been crushed by brutal words or deeds, and our response is, "He or she hurt me, broke my heart, used me, lied to me, took advantage of me, why should I ever forgive them?" You should forgive because, when you have been deeply hurt, forgiveness is the only way to truly be fair to yourself.

Let's set the scenario: You have been hurt. The unchangeable fact is that you have been wronged and you did not deserve it. You opened up your life and heart and let that person in, and he came in and stole from you, vandalized your emotions, raped your feelings when you didn't merit it. The following is the key to forgiveness: You've already been hurt one time. Why should you go the rest of your life experiencing the same hurt over and over again?

If there is no forgiveness, the injured person is doomed to a long life replay of the pain. The pain is nursed and rehearsed, and the scab sits precariously on the wound, easily dislodged. That wound is reopened to infection again, and it never heals. Why? Because you won't forgive! You refuse to erase the debt that person you feel owes you.

Forgiveness is more for you than it is for the person who hurt you. It's your way to release what has happened to you. Why should you have a VCR in your head that your mind replays your hurt over and over again? Sometimes we are not quick to forgive because we make the mistake of thinking forgiveness means the other person gets off the hook. "They hurt me; they made me bleed, and, if I forgive them, they get off free plus they get to pass go and collect $200 dollars."

Well, first of all, the hook is not in them the hook is in you! It's sticking out of your chest; you're the one that is crying at night. You are the one that is locked in an emotional prison until you can't even trust people any more. You need to be set free!

Remember this. God will settle the score, and you will be vindicated either in time or eternity! But you need to bust out of your jail cell of misery and be set free. The key to your jailbreak is forgiveness.

Why do we find it so hard to forgive? I believe there are three misconceptions that surround forgiveness:

3. To Forgive Means To Forget

Somebody says, "I forgive, but I can't forget." Then someone else says, "Well, then you haven't really forgiven." I don't know what they really mean by this. If they mean somehow I get amnesia or my mind is wiped clean of the wrong done to me, that doesn't really make sense.

That would be like going up to Jesus and asking Him, "Did you ever know a guy named Judas Iscariot?" Jesus says, "No, I never heard of him." That's a lie! He remembers the last supper, the kiss, the garden and the thirty pieces of silver. But here is the difference: When we forgive, forgiveness makes sure that the hurtful event loses its grip on our minds and emotions. We remember, but it loses its dominion; and, we are not thrown into fits of rage and convulsions of emotional epilepsy because of the pain. I am set free indeed! I remember what you did to me, how you hurt my family and me and how you let me down, but the memory can't dominate me anymore.

Some of you have been carrying childhood pains—abuse, physical, emotional, and sexual. A very demented and wicked person abused you, and you were never able to have a stable relationship. However, the worse thing about the abuse is the bondage you have had to live with all your life. Some devastating lie was told on you, and it has wounded you so deeply. You need to be set free!

To forgive is not to forget! If you have a family member who is a known pedophile, you must forgive him. But it would be wise not to leave them to baby-sit your kids' when you go shopping. Forgive, but don't forget. Snakes don't change their nature. God does not expect you to set yourself up again.

Every year Israel remembered Egypt. They celebrated the victory. This celebration is called the Passover. Egypt had no more dominion over them!

4.   To Forgive Is To Sanction The Hurting Act

Just because you forgive doesn't mean you are in agreement with the person that has done you wrong. Lies, abuse, the tearing down of reputation, and other acts of carnality will never be justifiable actions. Just look at the day of crucifixion. Jesus gave His life freely to pay the debt of our sins. He even forgave the vile men who perpetrated this violent act. But what they did can never be justified as the right thing to do.

It is the Lord's place to bring vengeance if vengeance is the punishment required. It is our place to forgive and give God the opportunity to vindicate us and our reputation. When God forgives your sin, that doesn't mean He is in agreement with your sin. Forgiveness does not excuse mean and evil behavior.

5. Forgiveness Doesn't Mean Immediate Reconciliation

God does not expect you to have a face-to-face encounter with whomever has hurt you. You don't have to confront a person to forgive him; neither do you have to wait for that person to ask you. No one asked for forgiveness at the cross, except a dying thief, and he didn't have anything physically to do with Christ's crucifixion. Yet Jesus prayed for the forgiveness of His tormentors. You cannot pray for your enemy's forgiveness until you have forgiven them.

No Pharisee called out, "We're sorry Jesus. We were wrong; you are the Son of God!" They reviled Him and mocked Him, and nobody asked for forgiveness. However, He said, "Father forgive them for they know not what they do." Just because you forgive doesn't mean you are going to embrace and sit down with your offender today.

Forgiveness is more for the person that has been hurt than the one that caused the pain. It allows you to move on with your life. If you don't forgive, the devil will keep you on a treadmill, and you will never make any progress. You don't have to see that person you forgave. I have forgiven some people that I'd rather not see. I don't want to socialize with them in my house. I'm not looking for a social relationship. Forgiveness is not intended to make intimate relational partners. You have to move on from where you are because you can't turn back time and be what you used to be to each other. Now, when we do forgive, three things happen to us:

6.   We begin to change our perception of the person who hurt us

When the hurt feeling is fresh we make that person the embodiment of evil or the devil incarnate. We engage in characterizing using broad strokes, something like, "That no- good-lousy dog," or "That devil. If they caught on fire, I wouldn't take the time to spit on them to put them out." We use expansive, hurtful words to characterize that person. We don't try to think objectively or clear-headed about them because the pain is so great we can't think clearly. All we know is, "You hurt me, and I hate you."

When we forgive, we begin to change our perception. We no longer see just the villains; we see them, as they really are—weak, sinful, frail, and fleshly. They are just like us without God's power and grace! So no longer are they just an object of our anger; they become the object of our prayers and sympathy for their weak minds. Pray for your enemies. They need deliverance, a touch from God, and a word of love from God.

7.   The feelings about that person are healed

Let's face it. Everyone has reasons to be bitter. Everyone has reasons and good reasons! Forgiveness starts the healing progression. This doesn't mean your feelings will jump from hatred to admiration the minute you choose to forgive. They just begin to move away from the negative toward the positive until the anger is no longer ripping you apart. This process can take years, but the first step on the road to healing must begin now. Rehab is a tough and long drawn out process. Time is on your side, and so is the Lord!

8.   We surrender our right to get even

The law of Mosses appeals to us—an eye for an eye and a tooth for a tooth—but if we were guilty in following the law to the extreme, we would live in a world full of blind, toothless people. We have to stop somewhere and forget settling the score. How many Jews and Arabs have to die? How many Catholics and Protestants in Northern Ireland have to die before they are satisfied? When does the score-keeping end? It's got to stop with somebody! When you say, "I will no longer worry about getting even," you are then on your way to a full and complete recovery.

In the city of Chicago there was a young couple with a seven-year-old daughter. They were a perfect, middle class family with a beautiful home and two new cars. The husband had a responsible job, worked hard, and was blessed. They were committed, Christian people that were totally plugged into their local church. They were young and beautiful, faithful people. In the course of driving home from the office the husband was hit head on by a drunk driver and was tragically and instantly killed. The wife was devastated, and her whole life changed. She became overwhelmingly bitter, mad at God, and unforgiving of the drunk driver, who like many survived the ordeal. She stopped going to church, and she developed impenetrable shell. Nobody could reach her. All she thought she had to live for was her daughter. She and her daughter were grocery shopping one day. They had a bag in the cart, and the mother and the little girl picked it up at the same time. They got into a little tug of war, and the little girl said, "Mommy, I can't do it if you won't let it go!" At that very moment the Holy Spirit spoke to her and the gloom was broken as God said, "I can't do it if you won't let it go!"

That's what God is saying to you! "Let it go, and I'll do it! I'll handle it, I will carry your load!" "Casting all your care upon him; for he careth for you" (I Peter 5:7). There is an old hymn that says, "I must tell Jesus... I can not bear these burdens alone." There are some things in life too heavy to carry! Give them to Jesus and let Him heal you, and you won't have to carry them any more. It is true you can't live life without an eraser. Get a good eraser (just make sure you do not steal it from your classmate; the end doesn't justify the means) and erase the mistakes of your past and erase the mistakes of others that have left a cruel mark on you, and be free.

CHAPTER THREE

RETROACTIVE RIGHTEOUSNESS

GRACE IS BY definition a clear act of forgiveness with no strings attached. Jesus makes us righteous by becoming our righteousness for us: "For he hath made him [to be] sin for us, who knew no sin; that we might be made the righteousness of God in him" (II Corinthians 5:21). Grace is definitely not what we deserve, but it is what we get. With the inherent weakness of mankind we fall short, everyday of our lives. Strive as we will, the mark is not quite hit. But thanks be unto God! Where we fall short, His grace makes it up and closes the gap by the power of the cross. The cross of Jesus Christ is the equalizer, and His grace forever flows. The miracle is in the fact that the river is not only lunging forward into time but also flowing backward into history. God's grace is retroactive in its power.

The word "retroactive" simply means, "having application to or effect on things prior to its enactment or going into effect as of a specified date in the past." Let me give you an example: Your employer says to you, "You deserve a raise which should start today. However, you are such a good employee that as a bonus we are going to make your raise retroactive as of January first." Then he turns to the secretary and tells her to cut you a check for six months back pay. Maybe you're thinking, "That would be more than retroactive; that would be a divine miracle if you knew my boss like I do."

For eyes to see, there is another miracle. Do you have sins in your past? Things that may be too horrific to even talk about? Has guilt been a ball and chain that doesn't seem to disappear with the passing of years? God through the power of the blood of Jesus Christ, reaches to the highest mountain and flows to the lowest valley, tracks sin to its most hidden lair and back to that dark depressing day that you call your past, the day you sinned, and sets you free! He sets you free from

> The Past of Sin
> The Power of Sin
> The Penalty of Sin.

You don't have to live one more day under the condemnation of sin!

I have heard people with pure motives and questioning eyes recite "But you don't know what I have done." You are right. But I don't have to know what you have done. I mean this with all respect I don't even want to know what you have done. God's grace doesn't revolve around what you have done. His grace is exclusively about what He has done. He has forgiven you of the past so you can live in the present and look forward to the future.

I heard a story that in an eccentric way reminds me of Christ's grace. A truck driver stopped at a little roadside café to grab a quick bite to eat on route to deliver the load of his big eighteen-wheeler. While sitting there enjoying a greasy cheeseburger and a cup of coffee, the man heard the ringing bell of the door opening. In walked a mean motorcycle gang, bent on trouble. The leader grabbed the truck driver and began to work him over, and, after he satisfied his hunger for inflicting pain, he shoved him to the next man who went to work. After the last man of the gang was finished, the last man took the poor truck driver by the seat of the pants and the nape of the neck, threw him out of the café, closed the door and sat down. They listened as the big truck pulled away. With a laugh of satisfaction the leader remarked snidely, "That ole boy wasn't much of a fighter, was he?" The cook, clad in a white tee shirt and soiled apron replied, "No, he sure wasn't, but he's not much of a good truck driver either; he just ran over eighteen motorcycles."

We in our own strength, wisdom, and will are no match for the devil. Before we were saved we were given the treatment of a slave. But now we have been given the keys to the kingdom to climb up in the Master's chariot and by God's grace the power to roll over every demon out of hell especially over those spirits that are always present to remind you of the past!

I saw a bumper sticker that puts things in perspective: "When the devil reminds you of your past, remind him of his future!" Forgiveness is supernatural, satisfying, and, oh, how sweet!

Look at the classic confession found in Psalms 51:1–13:

> To the chief Musician, A Psalm of David, when Nathan the prophet came unto him, after he had gone in to Bathsheba. Have mercy upon me, O God, according to thy lovingkindness: according unto the multitude of thy tender mercies blot out my transgressions. Wash me thoroughly from mine iniquity, and cleanse me from my sin. For I acknowledge my transgressions: and my sin is ever before me. Against thee, thee only, have I sinned, and done this evil in thy sight: that thou mightest be justified when thou speakest, and be clear when thou judgest. Behold, I was shapen in iniquity; and in sin did my mother conceive me. Behold, thou desirest truth in the inward parts: and in the hidden part thou shalt make

me to know wisdom. Purge me with hyssop, and I shall be clean: wash me, and I shall be whiter than snow. Make me to hear joy and gladness; that the bones which thou hast broken may rejoice. Hide thy face from my sins, and blot out all mine iniquities. Create in me a clean hear O God; and renew a right spirit within me. Cast me not away from thy presence; and take not thy holy spirit from me. Restore unto me the joy of thy salvation; and uphold me with thy free spirit. Then will I teach transgressors thy ways; and sinners shall be converted unto thee.

King David had, no doubt, committed a horrible act of sin, and there was no escape either by confession or by creed. David's sin falls under the prescribed elements of a crime, as follows:

1. The crime must be done voluntarily & intentionally.
2. The person must be legally capable of committing the crime.
3. There must be a law established prohibiting the action.
4. There must be a prescribed punishment.
5. The State or the Nation must have the ability to enforce the law.

The prophet of God had pointed him out and proclaimed in a thunderous tone that rattled every window in the kingdom, "Thou art the man!" David stands there a condemned, murderous adulterer without one hope of acquittal. Instead of pleading his case he cries for grace and mercy. What he is really asking for is for God to destroy the file marked "David, King of Israel: Sin Record." Can you imagine what David wants? He is asking God to forgive and forget, just to destroy the record, to burn the evidence, and to act as though it never happened.

If the President of the United States had an individual murdered just so he could commit adultery with the man's wife and the F.B.I.

revealed it, what do you think the consequences would be? I realize Presidents of the past have gotten away with a lot of crimes and sins. It is realistic to believe some probably have gotten away with murder and adultery. But if their crime was exposed in such away that their guilt was beyond reasonable doubt, even an act of Congress couldn't shred the evidence and destroy all the records. Without a doubt, conviction would surely come. Yet this is what David is asking for in his prayer. Hear the quiver in his voice: "O God have mercy on me! Blot out my sins! When I should be happy, I'm not. My sin is too dark. My past is too deep, and I have lost my joy of living. I thought I really wanted that sin, but, when I got it, it wasn't what I thought it would be. I lost what I had. Please forgive me!"

Is grace what David deserved? No, according to the Law (King or no King), his punishment was to be taken outside the city and given a rock concert in his honor. The punishment was a stoning.

I have another question. Do we deserve grace? No, we deserve the same fiery judgment the devil is going to get. That is why John Newton the author of "Amazing Grace" once said, "When I get to heaven I shall see three wonders (1) Many people I didn't expect to be there, (2) Many people I expected there. (3) The greatest wonder of all will be to find myself there." When we come to the cross, we come as beggars and leave as kings. We come broken, and we leave made whole. We come with nothing and leave with everything! Thank God for a grace that reaches back in time and gives us hope for the future.

One day a man was dying, so he called for his neighbor to come quickly to his bedside. The dying man knew he was about to meet the Lord and wanted nothing to keep him out of heaven. So, when his neighbor entered into the room, he immediately called out from his sickbed, "John, will you forgive me for having held this grudge all these many years? I forgive you for doing me wrong."

"Sure, Bill," John said. They made small talk for the next fifteen minutes, and then John decided to leave. Just as he was about to go over the threshold, Bill hollered out, "John remember this. If by chance I get well, this don't count."

That illustrates how shallow our forgiveness really is. But not God's forgiveness. The water will evaporate from the ocean, and elephants will roost in trees before God changes His mind and goes back on His forgiveness.

Do you remember the darkest day of human experience, the twilight of our Lord's earthly ministry? Christ was dying on the cross, and parallel to Him was a thief. He wasn't a very good thief because he had been caught. His past had finally caught up with him, and death was the sentence. As he was hanging on the cross with just a few counted breaths left, his body was in horrific pain and misery. The crowd was gathered below him, and, as he looked through tormented eyes, he didn't see one familiar face.

The reality set in that he was going to die and that he was alone. There was a brief thought of his mother and distant land called childhood, but it was suddenly taken from him as a maddening pain went through his broken body like a shock wave. He groaned and gritted his teeth with force enough to break his molars.

He heard the motley crowd that had only come to get their kicks in watching three men die, but their words were a blur. In the distance he heard the undomesticated dogs of Judea howl as their taste buds were tantalized by the smell of fresh human blood.

Then he turned his head ever so slightly to his left, and his eyes met the eyes of the Savior. It is as though time stood still for just one brief moment. He saw something in the eyes of Jesus that he had spent his lifetime looking for. The pain was forgotten for a moment, and a new hope burst forth upon his soul.

Something is right with this picture! His old dead, hard-callused heart felt the breath of life surge through it. All the hate dissipated, and love was resurrected. Then he said within himself, "Wait just a minute, this is the Son of God! All my life I have been at the wrong place at the wrong time, and now for one time in my life I am at the right place at the right time! I'm going to die; there is no getting around that, but what a deal: I am going to die beside the Savior of the world." Then he cries out in faith, "Lord I believe!" "Please remember me when you come into your kingdom."

Now here lies the problem: In order for Jesus to **remember** him the Lord must first **forget** this man's past. This man admitted his torrid past and threw himself on the mercies of God before the door of opportunity shut for eternity. The Lord said, "This day you shall be with me in paradise." Saved in the nick of time!

One sunny day an elderly lady was taking a leisurely walk by a pond when to her amazement, a frog jumped into her path, looked up, and began to beg for mercy. The frog said, "Please, lady, release me from this curse. For I was turned into an ugly frog, but I am really a handsome young prince. If you will kiss me, I will return to my original form, and we can get married and live happily ever after." The old woman reached down and picked up the frog and placed him in her purse. The frog protested, "Aren't you going to kiss me?" She replied, "Are you kidding? At my age, a talking frog is worth more than a young prince!"

There is only one power that can turn a thief into a prince, make a harlot holy, and a prostitute pure—the explosive power of God's grace! It can reach into your past, supernaturally jerk every skeleton out of the closet, shut the door ever so gently, crush those skeletons to fine powder, and then turn to you and say, "Where are thy accusers? Neither do I condemn thee; go and sin no more" (John 8:11). This is God's grace, retroactive grace.

Jesus blotted out our sins by nailing them to the cross. The cross is the greatest theme throughout the universe. Grand are the dim lit candles above, but grander is the cross. Spinning planets, streaking fire in the sky, suns, stars, and comets will one day burn out; but the eternal flame of the cross will burn forever. The storm of sin that began in a garden had traveled cross ward through the generations and had infected the whole planet until at last it burst forth upon Calvary. There in the darkness of the storm and howling winds a voice penetrated the blackness, "It is finished." And suddenly the curse was broken; the storm that came in like a lion went out like a lamb. All that was left was calm and sunshine for those who believe.

A traveler had booked passage on a ship that was bound for his beloved homeland. He went below and fell fast asleep. After several hours he awoke, got up, and went back to the deck. Looking over the starboard side, he saw a violent storm in the distance, and it frightened him. He turned to a sailor and said, "Do you think we can survive that storm?" The sailor smiled and replied, "Sir, don't be afraid of that storm because that storm will never touch us; it's already past!"

As a Christian there should never be a concern for the judgment of sin because it is already past. The judgment fell at Calvary. The cross is a bridge that stretches from time into eternity. Is grace what we deserve? No, and a thousand times no! But grace is what we get the hour we first believe.

I have friend who is head of security at a large Bible college and mega church. His name is Larry Johnson. One day I went to see him, and he gave me the VIP tour of the entire complex. Then he took me to the campus bookstore. He told me to get anything I wanted at his expense.

I didn't want to appear as though I was taking advantage of my friend, so I found a book or two that I really wanted and brought them to him. He looked at me and said, "You mean that's all you're going to get?" Then he said, "Come with me."

We went to the front counter, and he asked the clerk for a couple of brown paper bags. Then, taking me down the aisles, he asked, "Do you have this one"? "No, I replied." He filled both paper bags. You could not get another book in those two bags. As we exited the door, Larry turned to the clerk and said, "Put this on my tab." The clerk replied, "Yes, sir, Mr. Johnson!"

He paid the debt, and I got the benefit! In just the same way Christ paid the debt of sin, and I got the benefit of salvation. "Blessed be the Lord, who daily loadeth us with benefits, even the God of our salvation. Selah" (Psalms 68:19).

CHAPTER FOUR

SUPER SINNERS NEED SUPER GRACE

DO YOU EVER feel unworthy? Do you ever feel undeserving of God's grace? Welcome to the club! Our faithful (yet he feels unfaithful) President couldn't be with us today because he has already crossed over to the other side, but he did leave us his creed: "This [is] a faithful saying, and worthy of all acceptation, that Christ Jesus came into the world to save sinners; of whom I am chief" (I Timothy 1:15). Yes, President Paul really felt that way. Notice he did not use the past tense but rather the present tense. When he says "I am chief." When the height, depth, and width of God's holiness and His love begin to come into focus, you are left with only one question, "Who am I?" Then, the reality sets in: "I am a super sinner."

When we compare our righteousness to His righteousness, we come up short—like the distance between earth and the farthest star in the last sector of the universe. "But we are all as an unclean [thing], and all our righteousnesses [are] as filthy rags; and we all do fade as a leaf; and our iniquities, like the wind, have taken us away" (Isaiah 64:6). No matter how hard we try, we still collapse short.

Let's do a little imaginary experiment: Let's put every human being on the face of the earth on the coast of California and tell them to jump in and swim to Hawaii. How far do you think they would get? Some would be able to swim a few feet. Strong swimmers would be able to swim for many miles. But in the end, nobody would make it. Every last one would eventually be drowned if not eaten by sharks, no matter how fast and how strongly he could swim. To swim to Hawaii would be asking too much because it is impossible.

Likewise, for you to think you can get from earth to heaven by your own righteousness is just as impossible. It's not going to happen. Some churches offer swimming lessons, but what we need is not swimming lessons; what we need is a boat.

Here is some terrific news that has nothing to do with saving tons of money on your car insurance: Jesus is the Boat! When you can't reach God, He can reach you. When you can't touch God, He can touch you. When you can't find God, He can find you. This ability of God is called grace. Grace is so much more than God's unmerited favor.

Like the religious Pharisees of Jesus's day we tend to put more emphasis on what we do for God than on what God has done for us. Some people's favorite scripture is, "God helps those who help themselves." Not only is that not a scripture, it is not entirely true. Thank God He helps the helpless, the undeserving, those who do not measure up, and those who fail to achieve His standard. This is grace!

God's grace is a free gift! This may come as a shock, especially if you are from a Pharisaical background. You are a sinner before the Cross, and you are a sinner after the Cross. Take it: You don't have to stay on the boat, and if you so desire, with your free will, you can jump overboard and try to swim. However, you will never make it. Noah was saved by grace, but he wasn't held hostage on the ark. God shut the door, but

Noah could have climbed out the window. God controlled the door, and Noah controlled the window.

I once met five men who were out witnessing their faith. I was at Richard Morgan's house visiting with his mom and dad, Joyce and Glenn. When the five men knocked on the door, Glenn invited them in. After about ten minutes we discovered their entire mission was not to find the unchurched but to proselyte the people who were already faithful members. Their argument was that no matter what church one went to, it was the wrong church. Their church was the only true church because they were the only ones who taught the real truth. To them the real truth was this: After you are saved you must be sanctified, and, once you are sanctified, you will never sin again. After they made their belief and purpose clear, I causally asked one of them, "You mean you have never sinned ever since you were sanctified?"

"That is what we are trying to tell you," he replied.

"Well, you just committed your first sin," I said.

"What do you mean?" he asked.

"You just lied and you are a liar!" I exclaimed.

He jumped up, turned red in the face, and shouted at me, "Don't you call me a liar!"

"Oops," I said, "There is your second sin you are getting mad and angry at me."

At this point. the leader of the group had to restrain the man. In about thirty seconds, they were all going out the door.

What part of "sinner" don't you understand? Sinners need a Savior—not just yesterday or today but forever! Let's look at three scriptures. First, Romans 5:1,2,19: "Therefore being justified by faith, we have peace with God through our Lord Jesus Christ" (1). And: "By whom also we have access by faith into this grace wherein we stand, and rejoice in hope of the glory of God" (2). And third: "For as by one man's disobedience many were made sinners, so by the obedience of one shall many be made righteous" (19). One needs to read the whole chapter, but these three scriptures shine the light on an incredible truth. The only way to stand and to have peace, joy and hope is to be righteous before a holy God. We are not righteous. Therefore, we are not just up a creek without a paddle, but, remember, without a boat. However, verse nineteen says, "…that we have been made righteous through Jesus Christ." He is the boat, the only hope of eternal life!

In 2003 when I served as Chaplain for the Oklahoma House of Representatives at the State Capital in Oklahoma City, I gave those lawmakers a stirring devotional and direction for the day before I opened the session with prayer. In the course of my sermon I told this story, which is now a permanent record, forever in print in the *Oklahoma House Journal* at the State Capital:

> Years ago' when Muhammad Ali was at his height and, no doubt, the greatest heavy weight boxer of all time, he boarded an airplane.
>
> And after he was seated, the flight attendant came by and said,
>
> "Sir, you're going to have to put on your seatbelt now." He replied in his cocky, little attitude, "Ma'am Superman don't need no seatbelt!"
>
> She then looked at him and said, "Sir, Superman don't need no airplane."

You are no Superman, and neither am I. Like Paul we are super sinners and super sinners need super grace. As a matter of fact, let's take a test and find out which of the following best characterizes you:

Spiritual Efficiency:

1. I am faster than a speeding bullet.
2. I am almost as fast as a very slow bullet.

3. I am as fast as a still bullet.
4. I am as fast as the box the bullet came in.
5. I get wounded, shot in the leg, while attempting to shoot the bullet.

Spiritual Strength:

1. I am stronger than a locomotive.
2. I am stronger than the old conductor of a locomotive.
3. I am stronger than the luggage boy of a locomotive.
4. I am stronger than the luggage.
5. I am stronger than the smoke of a locomotive.

Spiritual Agility:

1. I can leap tall buildings with a single bound.
2. I can leap, would you believe, short buildings?
3. I must use a trampoline to leap over buildings.
4. I can leap over only imaginary buildings.
5. I can run through a window on first floor of building.

Is it a bird? Is it a plane? No, it's Super Sinner that is in dire need of a Super Savior with Super Grace. We all need God's grace! We need it because we are not Superman with super powers to always be at the right place at the right time, to solve all the problems, to right all the wrongs, to always save the day, and to always rescue every damsel in distress. Paul asked for a miracle, but God gave him grace: "For this thing I besought the Lord thrice, that it might depart from me. And he said unto me, My grace is sufficient for thee: for my strength is made perfect in weakness" (II Corinthians 12:8–9).

What does it mean that God's grace is "sufficient"? It accurately means there is like the wings of the angels that were seated upon the ancient Ark of the Covenant; they covered the ark, much like buying a meal for a friend; when they try to pay, you say, "I have you covered." In other words, I have already paid for it, and your money is no good.

Can you imagine sitting with your five-year-old daughter at a restaurant, and after the meal, she reaches over and gives you fifty cents and says, "Here, daddy, I want to buy my own lunch." If you are like me, there are three reactions that come to mind:

1. It is my responsibility not yours.
2. Fifty cents won't buy it.
3. You only have the fifty cents because I gave it to you.

We are God's children, and we are totally dependent upon Him; no questions asked, we are. It is his responsibility to save us because we can't save ourselves. We sure can't buy our salvation; it costs too much. Besides, anything we could give the Lord, He gave to us in the first place. He has us covered; I mean, literally, He has us covered! Think of it this way: Sin put you in prison, and you were guilty. Above everything else you were guilty of crucifying Jesus, but Jesus rose from the dead, came to where you were, paid your bail, dropped all charges, pardoned you, then took you home and adopted you as His child. "So shall you forever be with the Lord."

One can never exhaust God's grace. Why was it that when we were lost, confused, and alienated from God, we came to Him and found the sufficiency of His amazing grace and gladly accepted it? Now since we have experienced it and lived in it for some time, do we start believing that somehow God's grace has started to lose its power? As though somehow in our imperfection we will eventually liquidate all of God's grace? When will we ever get it through our thick heads that it is not about our weakness, it's all about His strength? You will always be weak, and He will always be strong.

You cannot exhaust God's grace. Could you imagine two small minnows swimming in the vastness of the Atlantic Ocean worried that they might drink the Atlantic Ocean dry? Or, two small sparrows worried to the point of a nervous breakdown that they might use all the oxygen that is in the immeasurable sky? God says to the minnows, "Go ahead and swim and drink all you want. My ocean is sufficient," and, to the sparrows He says, "Breathe and fly on, little birds. My sky is sufficient." I have a word from God to you: "My grace is sufficient!"

Gold and diamond mines are eventually raped of their precious contents. Oil wells one day have no more oil to give and the rocking arms on their pumps stop siphoning. The pumps become a part of the landscape that point back in time to a more prosperous era.

The coal mines that once clamored with activity in some rural countryside are now calm, dark and silent. All that can be heard is the rustling of the leaves as an occasional gust of wind comes blowing through. The men are gone; the machinery is gone. Why? The coal is gone. The demand has depleted the supply.

However, the riches of God's grace are inexhaustible. Every human being that has gone before us on this journey has in no way made His grace less. God's grace is an inexhaustible supply for time and eternity. After God has supplied grace to the unborn millions, when the last of Adam's race stands lonesome by the fountain of grace, it will be as full as the day the first Adam was invited to drink, live, wash, and be clean.

It is like the fishes and the loaves at the feeding of the five thousand; they just kept on coming out of the lad's sack.

It is like the first miracle Jesus did at the wedding in Cana of Galilee. The hosts ran out of wine, but Jesus demonstrated the sufficiency of His supply; he showed that it never runs out. His grace is always available 24/7.

Any person, any place, at any time can call upon the Lord and find His grace a living flowing fountain: "For whosoever shall call upon the name of the Lord shall be saved" (Romans 10:13).

That brings us to five important pivotal points:

1. You can't get to heaven without God's grace (you have no boat of your own).

2. You don't deserve God's grace (you killed God's only Son).

3. You didn't or cannot make yourself righteous (you were made righteous by Him).

4. You can't exhaust God's grace (you don't have enough time or eternities).

5. You cannot buy God's grace (you don't have enough money or resources).

There is not enough money in the Federal Reserve, Fort Knox, the World Bank or all the banks in the entire world to pay for just one drop of Jesus' blood. The worlds wealth is not enough!

Let us look at this from another perspective. Just yesterday a sweet lady in our church gave me three authentic Confederate bills, one for one dollar, one for five dollars and one for ten dollars. Later I called a coin collector to get some idea how much they are worth. He told me that dependent upon their condition (which I believe is excellent) they would value between twenty-five to forty dollars. I was shocked for I thought they were worth much more. The reason that their value is so low is not their age or the fact that they were from the Confederacy but simply due to supply and demand. There is not a great demand, and the supply, believe it or not, is plenteous. What makes an article valuable is great demand and short supply.

Every person who has ever lived on this peopled planet is in need of a Savior. That makes the demand as high as it can possibly get. Now, there is only one Savior, and His name is Jesus Christ, not ten, not two, but only one: "Neither is there salvation in any other: for there is none other name under heaven given among men, whereby we must be saved" (Acts 4:12). Clearly, the supply is limited only to Jesus.

Diamonds, rubies and emeralds are called precious stones because of the limited supply. Gold and silver are categorized as precious metals, again, because of the lack of them. There are rocks by the millions lying everywhere, but they are of no value and are definitely not called precious rocks.

The less there is of an object the more valuable and the more precious that object becomes. If everyone in the world was dying of a bacterial germ, and there was only one vial of antidote, how much would be that antidote be worth? I believe I would safe in saying "Priceless."

Now do you understand why the Bible says, "Forasmuch as ye know that ye were not redeemed with corruptible things, [as] silver and gold, from your vain conversation [received] by tradition from your fathers; But with the **precious blood of Christ**, as of a lamb without blemish and without spot" (I Peter 1:18–19)?

In I Peter 2:7, Peter writes, speaking of Jesus, "He is precious." "Precious" does not mean He is just lovely and sweet like the description of a grandchild. He is the only Savior who came from another world with the only blood antidote for sin. His blood is the real deal; it is the only blood that can save the human race, because He is the only Savior given to the human race by God the Father and He offers salvation free to those who will accept Him as the only Lord of their lives.

Let's say you are in a burning building on the seventeenth floor, and the possibility of escape is zero. As you are moving away from the flames and choking smoke, you realize you have two choices: You can either burn in the flame, or you can jump from the window to a certain death. Death is the only option you have, but your choice of the way you will die is up to you. You finally decide that rather than roast to death in a tormenting flame, you might as well go out in style and jump from the window. So you climb out onto the ledge, but just as you muster enough courage to jump, something amazing happens. A large man with a blue suit that has an "S" on the chest hovers in front of you in midair. His red cape is flapping in the breeze. He looks into your eyes and speaks with a mastery that calms your fears: "Don't be afraid because I am here to save you,"

"Who are you?" you ask.

"I'm Superman!" he replies.

You have questions:

"How can you stand in midair? Are you sure you can save me? You do look strong, but are you absolutely sure you can support both your and my weight? How can I believe you really are Superman?"

The Man of Steel just smiles and says, "Don't worry, I am Superman. My super powers are enough so just jump and let's get out of here!"

There are only two things necessary for your survival, faith and works: You must believe he is Superman, and your faith must motivate you enough to jump and cling to him as the only hope of your salvation (salvation meaning deliverance from the burning building). We are in a burning building and time is running out. But how often do we stop to ask questions? "Lord, are You sure You can save me? You just don't realize how weighted down with sin I really am. Is the blood really enough? Lord, are you really the Savior?"

Jesus just smiles and says, "Don't worry, my child. I am the Savior, and I have all power in heaven and in earth. So don't let your heart be troubled; just believe, jump, and cling to me. I am all you need!"

Friend, you don't need Superman; you need a Supernatural Man. Jesus Christ is a Supernatural Savior! And for super sinners, super grace is always available.

CHAPTER FIVE

THE HUMPTY DUMPTY DILEMMA

***

THE REAL ESSENCE of the Christian teaching is the search for wholeness. Every one of us must concede the devastating effects of brokenness and our inability to put all the pieces back together again. We are acquainted with brokenness—broken relationships, broken bodies, broken dreams, broken hopes, and, most of all broken souls. The impossibility of saving ourselves is a cold hard fact. The fall of Adam broke our fellowship with God, and we were alienated from Him. All of us were born broken people. I am convinced that the irresistible magnetism of the Gospel is its message that our Humpty Dumpty destinies can be escaped. No doubt you will remember the following nursery rhyme:

> Humpty Dumpty sat on the wall;
> Humpty Dumpty had a great fall.
> All the king's horses and all the king's men
> Couldn't put Humpty Dumpty back together again.

Now the real problem is that the king's horses and the king's men took Humpty Dumpty to the wrong source of healing. First and foremost, it was evident Humpty Dumpty was in no position to help or save himself. And, secondly, the king's horses and the king's men couldn't find a cure to put Humpty back together again. Humpty was unable to effect a change in his situation. The king's horses have failed and the king's men have also been unsuccessful. Why? This was a job for the King! And, had they gone to the King, Humpty Dumpty would still be around (no pun intended) today.

> Jesus Christ came to our wall;
> Jesus Christ died for our fall.
> So in spite of death and regardless of sin
> Through His grace He puts us back together again!

When Bill Clinton was the president of the free world, I was at times mistaken for the Commander-in-Chief. Now, I honestly am not saying this for prides sake. It is my personal feeling, as well as my wife Keleta's that there is a micro-resemblance, but I really don't look like Mr. Clinton. I have been involved as a police chaplain for years, and on one occasion we were patrolling a neighborhood. As we passed a house with a crowd of people sitting in the front yard, one lady jumped up and started screaming and waving her arms in the air to get our attention. I told the officer that I was with that there must be a problem, so we stopped and backed up. This dear woman came right up to the window, looked in and stared at me, then blurted out in her southern draw "Oh! I thought you were the President!" She laughed when I replied, "Lady, on my worst day, at three o'clock in the morning, with the flu, I still look better than Bill Clinton looked at the Presidential Inaugural Ball!"

My point is, when someone mistakes me for Bill Clinton, he or she has a bad case of mistaken identity. But there is a worse case of mistaken identity when God reaches way down in the miry pit of sin and picks up dirty filthy sinners on their way to hell, saves them, sanctifies them, and fills them with His Spirit, and those individuals put on a self-righteous mask and act as though everyone must live up to their standards. Somehow these twenty-first century Pharisees have a twisted misconception. They have been fooled into believing that they are God. They run around and act like God died and left them in charge. They have even changed the Scripture to read, "And whosoever was not found living exactly like Bro. Holy Joe was cast into the lake of fire." They are so narrow-minded that, if a mosquito hit them between the eyes, it would put out both their eyes! The Bible is very clear: There is only one-way to heaven. And it is not my way, your way, man's way, the Assemblies of God way, the Baptist way, or the Catholic way. It is God's way. It's the Calvary way. It's the Blood bought way, and it's the Cross way.

God is so far beyond us. He is nothing like us who are good and bad. We mess up. We foul up. We are inconsistent, and we make mistakes. But, not God! He has never made one mistake. He has never been late. He is always on time. God is always consistent, always holy, always good, always right, and He is never wrong! Wake up and smell the espresso latté, man.

You and I cannot save ourselves. If we could, as the apostle Paul said, "Then the cross was in vain" (Galatians 2:21). If you and I had the transcendent power to save ourselves, then God made the biggest blunder of the universe by sending His only begotten Son to this earth to die for our sins. You cannot save yourself any more than a hippopotamus can jump to the moon on a pogo stick. It is impossible to save yourself. This is the reason God sent His only Son to this sin-infected planet to save those who could not save themselves.

The cobra is one of the world's most poisonous snakes. For centuries the bite of a cobra meant sure and sudden death. The country of India is highly populated with these venomous serpents and, when men were bitten, they died a quick, painful death. The bite of a cobra was the death sentence.

THERE WAS ONLY ONE PERFECT MAN WHO EVER LIVED
THE REST OF US HAVE TO SWIM

One day the government of India discovered a certain stock of Belgium horse that was immune to the deadly venom of the cobra. When bitten, the horse got a little sick, but he did not die. There was something in that horse's blood that made him immune. So, they took the blood of a cobra—bitten horse and created anti-venom, a serum that would immunize anyone who was bitten by a cobra. No longer was the bite of the cobra the sentence of death. Because of the anti-venom produced from the blood of the Belgium horse, death by cobra bite had been annulled.

God created a garden and placed man in it. Man was told he could eat of every tree of the garden except one, the tree of good and evil. The serpent deceived man, and he disobeyed God. The day man ate the fruit death entered into this world. Man had been bitten by a serpent more poisonous than a cobra, and for thousands of years death reigned. We all had to die because we were all born into sin and we all died in sin.

There was no antidote, no serum or anti-venom. The whole human race was polluted by sin, and the poison was in our bloodstream. Death was inevitable. We all had to die. We lived with the death sentence because the serpent bit us.

But two thousand years ago there came One who was immune to the bite of the snake. His name is Jesus Christ. He was immune because He had no sin. His blood was pure and precious. To save the human race from death He willfully allowed the serpent to bite Him, and He, who knew no sin, became sin that we might become the righteousness of God.

Jesus said, "Devil, inoculate me with the sins of the world, and in my death I will conquer death, sin and you. My blood will become the anti-venom to those who have been bitten by the snake."

Thank God, there is a hope! His blood is not a cheap, patented medicine; it is an eternal cure for those who cannot save themselves. "But if we walk in the light, as he is in the light, we have fellowship one with another, and the blood of Jesus Christ his Son cleanseth us from all sin" (I John 1:7).

The apostle Paul writes in the fifth chapter of Galatians:

> Stand fast therefore in the liberty wherewith Christ hath made us free, and be not entangled again with the yoke of bondage. Behold, I Paul say unto you, that if ye be circumcised, Christ shall profit you nothing. For I testify again to every man that is circumcised, that he is a debtor to do the whole law. Christ is become of no effect unto you, whosoever of you are justified by the law; ye are fallen from grace. For we through the Spirit wait for the hope of righteousness by faith. For in Jesus Christ neither circumcision availeth any thing, nor uncircumcision; but faith which worketh by love.
>
> Ye did run well; who did hinder you that ye should not obey the truth? This persuasion cometh not of him that calleth you (Galatians 5:1–8).

Remember this: If you are depending on the Law (good works) to save you, then you must keep the Law and not be guilty in breaking it at any point. You will be judged by it, and to break it at any one minor point is to break it all.

Let me give you an example: You are returning from Portland, Oregon, to Miami, Florida, which is 3,268 miles away. You get within ten miles of the city limit sign, and suddenly you are pulled over by a policeman for speeding. You say, "Officer I have kept the speed limit all the way from Portland, Oregon. For three thousand, two hundred and fifty eight miles I have not went over the speed limit not even one mile an hour over, so please don't write me a ticket." He replies, "I appreciate all the miles you have driven successfully without incident or breaking the law. But three thousand, two hundred and fifty eight miles is not enough. You have to go three thousand, two hundred and sixty eight miles without going over the limit. Here is your ticket, sir. You have a nice day."

If when you stand in the judgment, you want "works" to be your defense attorney, then have at it. But, again, remember, you will be judged accordingly.

In lifeguard training, I am told students are taught they should never try to save an individual until the individual quits trying to save himself. Otherwise, it is very possible that the lifeguard could become a victim also. Grace saves you when you quit trying to save yourself. Simply trust Jesus and His finished work on the cross. At that point grace dives into the cesspool of sin, pulls you to shore, and breathes into your nostrils the breath of life; you then become a living soul, a quickening spirit, and you start life brand new and all over again. Literally, a new creature emerges and old things pass away.

This act of grace is similar to what happened to the apostle Peter on that dark, stormy night when he tried to walk on the water. After taking his eyes off of Jesus, he was totally mesmerized by the wind and the waves, and, beginning to sink, he cried out in the darkness, "Jesus save me!" Immediately Jesus reached down and pulled him back up.

Paul wrote the book of Galatians to combat the teachings of the Judaizers (a group of legalistic gospel-perverting Jews). I guess, you could call them the king's horses and the king's men; however, they were more like the king's donkeys. They came to Galatia teaching that Gentiles must put themselves back under the bondage of the law to be saved. To fully understand who the Judaizers were one must go back to Genesis and revisit the story of Cain and Abel. Adam, their father, instructed both of his sons in the proper approach to God and the promise of the coming Messiah, Jesus Christ. It was through faith in blood atonement. After the fall they had sewed fig leaves (man's attempt) to cover themselves. But God killed animals and shed blood to make coats of skin to cover them. Abel's faith leaped the centuries to the Cross and made blood atonement for sin. Cain, on the other hand rejected the teaching of faith, grace, and blood atonement. Substituting good works in the place of blood, he was rejected at the altar.

The Judaizers taught salvation was purchased through good works instead of the blood of Christ. Their teaching becomes the burden of religion. Don't kid yourself: The Judaizers are still around today. They tell the world to come to Jesus, and they promise He will become the joy of their salvation. After the lost get saved, the Judaizers load them down with the burden of religion and then wonder why the new converts don't make it.

This reminds me of a funny story I heard about a man at Los Angeles International Airport who was worried about missing his plane: He had no wristwatch and could not locate a clock, so he hurried up to a total stranger and said, "Excuse me could you give me the time, please?"

The stranger smiled and said, "Sure."

He set down the two large suitcases he was carrying and looked at the watch on his wrist.

"It is exactly 5:09. The temperature outside is 72 degrees, and it is supposed to rain tonight. In Paris the sky is clear and the temperature is 34 degrees Celsius. The barometer reading there is 27.14 and falling. And, let's see, in Moscow the sun is shining brightly. Oh, by the way, the moon should be full tonight here in Los Angeles, and…"

"Your watch tells you all that?" The man interrupted.

"Oh, yes and much, much more. You see, I invented this watch, and, I can assure you, there is no other timepiece like it in the world."

"I want to buy that watch! I'll pay you one thousand dollars for it right now."

"No, it's not for sale," said the stranger as he reached down to pick up his suitcases.

"Wait! Five thousand. I'll pay you five thousand dollars, cash," offered the man, reaching for his wallet.

"No, I can't sell it. You see, I plan to give it to my son for his twenty-fifth birthday. I invented it for him to enjoy."

"Okay, listen, I'll give you ten thousand dollars. I've got the money right here."

The stranger paused. "Ten thousand? Well, okay. It's yours for ten thousand even."

The man was absolutely elated. He paid the stranger, took the watch, snapped it on his wrist with glee, and said "Thanks" as he turned to leave.

"Wait," said the stranger. With a big smile he handed the two heavy suitcases to the man and added, "Don't forget the batteries."

We tell people come to Jesus and experience joy, blessing, peace and forgiveness of sin. Then we load them down with all these man made regulations that are not found in the Bible.

> We turn faith into works
> Freedom into fetters
> Love into law
> Relationship into religion.

May I lay a revolutionary truth on you that can change your life? Something that the Judaizers left out, something the Pharisees left out, and something many so-called Christian churches have left out? God loves you! Out of all the things God could love, He loves you! He is perfect, and you are imperfect; and He loves you. He is pure, and you are impure; and He loves you. He loves you so much that He sent His Son to shed His blood to bathe you in what He was so you could come into His presence to commune with Him as though you were like Him.

If we depend on anything other than Christ crucified to save us from our sins, we have fallen from grace. We declare openly, "Jesus blood is not enough. " If God Himself could not get the job done on the Cross, then what other force in the universe has any hope to make the difference? Nothing I can add, no contribution I can make, no service I can render, will help my case on judgment day. Only Jesus, only Jesus!

There will inevitability come a moment in my life that time will fade into eternity, and alone I will stand before God Himself. And the books will be opened, and there, transparent as a pane of glass, my life will be open. No doubt, there is a list of sins that cover many pages. And in that moment, when I am given a chance to speak to the Judge, I will say, "Your Honor, guilty as charged. I am guilty on every account. But when I was sixteen years old, I got down on my knees and in repentance I asked Jesus, that is my attorney, into my heart. I was a sinner, and I needed a Savoir. It was at that very moment I believed Jesus paid the penalty for me and the Cross was not in vain." Then I will turn to Jesus and say, "Help me Lord, you are all I have!" And He will reply, "And I am all you need!" Then the verdict will fall, "Guilty! But forgiven!"

The patent truth is captured in the song, "Nothing but the Blood," written by Robert Lowry, a songwriter of another century:

1. What can wash away my sin?   Nothing but the blood of Jesus;

2. What can make me whole again?   Nothing but the blood of Jesus.

3. For my pardon this I see   Nothing but the blood of Jesus;

4. For my cleans-ing, this my plea   Nothing but the blood of Jesus.

5. Nothing can for sin atone   Nothing but the Blood of Jesus;

6. Naught of good that I have done   Nothing but the Blood of Jesus.

7. This is all my hope and peace   Nothing but the Blood of Jesus;

8. This is all my righteousness   Nothing but the Blood of Jesus.

THERE WAS ONLY ONE PERFECT MAN WHO EVER LIVED THE REST OF US HAVE TO SWIM

Chorus:

Oh precious is the flow that makes me white as snow;
no other fount I know, Nothing but the blood of Jesus.

Several years ago while attending Bible College a few friends and I were a little bored. It was Saturday, and you know teenagers: "action" is their middle name, even if they are all young preachers.

One of our instructors told us there was an interesting cave just outside of town and how to get there. Once we arrived, we discovered the cave was just as the professor had described. You entered through a small hole and walked 150 feet until you came to a dead end. Then you had to shimmy up a twelve-foot shaft and go further from there until you reached a large room. To exit you climbed out another hole coming outside on top of the hill. (In later years an ancient Indian burial ground was discovered in that site when the state of Missouri was widening the highway.) We began to frequent the cave regularly.

After a few visits I became moderately good at climbing up the twelve-foot shaft, climbing faster than the others. This caught the attention of my friend, Clifford Hurst, who started telling everyone at school of my extraordinary ability.

The tragedy is that I started believing my own fanfare. So each time we went to the cave, I tried to be a little more spectacular and pushed myself a little harder. One day there was a small crowd that came to conquer the cave. When we reached the shaft, being the expert climber, I told them I would be last and bring up the rear. Everyone there needed to see me in action from the topside I thought.

After I helped the last one up the shaft, it was the Legend's time to strut his stuff. I started climbing to the top with pride. But instead of feeling like a squirrel climbing a great oak tree, I felt more like a piece of lead sinking to the bottom of the lake. For some unknown reason I had lost all power in my limbs although I struggled with all my might. Just as

I neared the top and reached up to grab the ledge, it happened. I couldn't do it, so I just let go. But before I plummeted to the bottom, seeing it all happen, Mark Barker, a young man twice my size, grabbed my wrist and saved my life, or at least a broken leg or two.

He pulled me up and then commented, "Guy, you almost didn't make it. Do you know how close you came to falling?" I replied, "Better than you. I really thought I was gone. Thank you!"

I could have said, "Let go of me. I am the best there is when it comes to getting to the top. I am a legend (in my own mind)."

The Bible is plain. "Pride goeth before destruction, and an haughty spirit before a fall" (Proverbs 16:18). If you think you can climb to heaven in your own strength, on your own merit, or by your own good works, you are deceived. You are in for a great fall. You have literally fallen from grace. But the good news is that in your falling, God, with bigger hands and stronger arms, stands ready to immediately pull you up and keep you from falling.

God is waiting for you to commit the full weight of your life to the Cross. Salvation has nothing to do with your heritage, your name, or the name of your church. Salvation has everything to do with Christ, the King of Kings, and the simple proclamation of the naked truth; Jesus saves by His blood!

CHAPTER SIX

WHO WAS THAT MASKED MAN?

IF I LIVE to be a hundred, there'll never be a time when hearing those first few blasts of brass of the "William Tell Overture" won't take me back to my childhood, to a simpler time when I believed that there was a man who, with his Indian companion, was out there righting all the wrongs and teaching villains that greed and prejudice will fall before justice in the end. For me, the Saturday morning cowboys fanned the flame of imagination more than anything else. The Lone Ranger was one of the greatest heroes that ever rode through the legendary Wild West and across our television screen.

With a fiery horse at the speed of light, a cloud of dust, and a hearty, "Hi, Yo, Silver, Away!" the Lone Ranger rides again! With the Wisdom of Solomon, the grit of a pit bull, the courage of a lion tamer, and the keen mind of a Scotland Yard detective, he and Tonto always saved the day. With blazing silver guns and silver bullets the Lone Ranger and good ole faithful Tonto whip impossible odds. Then after a dozen or more "Me not know Kemosabe," this dynamic duo rides off into the sunset.

And the show usually closed with someone holding a silver bullet asking, "Who was that masked man?"

We live in a world of the artificial. At our disposal we have a catalog of imitations, of everything from hair to eyeballs, ice cream to chocolate bars, eggs to legs. Don't take me wrong; these are wonderful blessings of technology. But problems develop when people become artificial, when we hide behind a mask or superficial facade trying to conceal who we really are. Many reading this book right now are masked people. Some wear a religious mask; some wear a social mask, others wear an intellectual mask. To take those masks off for most people would be more terrifying than swimming with the Loch Ness Monster.

Everyday that you sport your mask, the mask becomes stronger and more binding. You are bound to the past, the present, and the future. Let me ask you: How would you like to live in the greatest dimension of sincerity you have ever known? How would you like to be totally free to rip off the mask and be not only who you are but also everything God wants you to be? Grace is such a wonderful, fantastic, magnificent, and breathtaking characteristic of God! Grace is the power to be free from all masks. Today is a new day; the Bible calls it the day of salvation.

In the coming judgment of God, nothing will be hid and every secret will be exposed. God gives fair warning, "But if ye will not do so, behold, ye have sinned against the LORD: and be sure your sin will find you out" (Numbers 32:23).

One hot, sultry evening two young men were driving down a county dirt road in an old Ford pickup, when the truck blew a radiator hose. They pulled over, evaluated the problem, and started walking to town. After they had walked about a mile, they came to a small farmhouse with a barn in the back. Behind the barn were several wrecked cars and trucks.

They walked up to the house and knocked on the door. An aged farmer came to the door and asked, "What can I help you boys with?"

One of the young men explained the dire straits they were in and asked if they could look for a hose in one of the junked cars behind the barn. The farmer said, "Sure, but before you go back there you have to know I have a big dog behind the barn. But don't pay any attention to him; his bark is worse than his bite. Oh, he'll make a lot of noise, but don't worry, he won't bite. He is all bluff."

The two young men went behind the barn and, while they were looking for a hose to fit their pickup, one of the boys discovered an open well. Being of the curious nature, he dropped a rock down the well to see how deep it was. He listened intently but never heard the water splash. So he excitedly yelled to his friend, "Hey, dude, come here! You are not going to believe this."

"Believe what?" his friend said.

"I dropped a rock down this well, and I never heard it hit the bottom. Man, this is a deep well." Then he said to his friend, "Go get that battery and let's drop it down the well."

They dropped the battery down the shaft and waited, and again they heard nothing. One said, "My word this is incredible. I wonder how deep this well is?"

He then turned and spotted a car block and got one of those great ideas, the kind you get when you are young and full of testosterone and empty of brains. "Here. Help me get that car block, and we will drop it down the well." So they pulled and pushed until they finally got the car block to the edge and with one more heave they pushed it off into the well.

As they waited again, the farmer's dog came out of nowhere growling like a tiger, with claws that seemed two inches long and canine fangs that seemed even longer. It was very apparent that this dog was mad and in great distress at the sight of the two young men. He kept coming closer and closer while the two adventure seekers were frozen in their tracks, remembering what the farmer had said and hoping the dog would call off his death pursuit at any moment. But he didn't. And just as he reached the two petrified teenagers, they stepped out of the way, and the dog fell down the well. They listened as his furious growl faded away never to be heard again.

They found a hose, and upon returning to the farmer's house, one of the boys got a guilty conscience and said, "You know, we have to tell the old farmer about his dog."

"I know but what will we tell him?"

"The truth," replied the instigator, and then he added, "Just not the whole truth."

They knocked again on the farmer's door, and again he came. "Did you boys find a hose to fit your truck?"

"Yes, sir, we did, but there is something we need to tell you. Your dog fell down that well back there."

"Oh, no, boys, not my dog."

"Sir, it was your dog."

"Boys, it couldn't have been my dog. Are you talking about a big German Shepherd about this tall, black and silver in color?"

"Yes, sir, that was him."

Then the farmer said, "No way, boys. I just know it could not have been my dog. My dog is tied up to an engine block!"

You can't hide your sin. It always has a bloodhound characteristic of tracking you down. You can only wear your mask so long. Then God reveals the man or women behind the mask.

Why do we wear masks? That is easy. To conceal our identity. We don't want people to see and know the person we are. The fear of being seen for who we really are, for some, far outweighs the fear of God to the point they just keep wearing ridiculous masks year after year. But God knows, and the sooner we fully understand that, the sooner we can be set free. God knows where you hid it, what you said, what you did, and what is in your heart. You may conceal your identity from men, but God sees you in the dark.

> And not as Moses, which put a veil over his face, that the children of Israel could not steadfastly look to the end of that which is abolished: But their minds were blinded:

for until this day remaineth the same vail untaken away in the reading of the old testament; which vail is done away in Christ. But even unto this day, when Moses is read, the vail is upon their heart. Nevertheless when it shall turn to the Lord, the vail shall be taken away. Now the Lord is that Spirit: and where the Spirit of the Lord is, there is liberty. But we all, with open face beholding as in a glass the glory of the Lord, are changed into the same image from glory to glory, even as by the Spirit of the Lord (I Corinthians 3:13–18).

This scripture makes it clear a "vail" is a mask, and masks close God out. Many Christians are performance-oriented. The most neglected truth in the Bible is God loves you. He really loves you, and you are not accepted because of your performance. You are accepted because of His love. If you were to look through glasses that have red lenses, you would see everything in the world red. The same would be true for blue, yellow, or pink. If you have accepted the blood atonement of Jesus Christ, then God sees you through the blood. When God looks at you, He sees Jesus. Jesus is your righteousness because you have none of your own. That is why it is so important to confess your sins. When you don't confess your sins, you hide behind a mask, and you literally shut out God and any hope for forgiveness. The great Apostle John (better known as the Apostle of Love) wrote, "If we say that we have no sin, we deceive ourselves, and the truth is not in us. If we confess our sins, he is faithful and just to forgive us our sins, and to cleanse us from all unrighteousness. If we say that we have not sinned, we make him a liar, and his word is not in us" (I John 1:8–10).

When you feel unworthy and condemned, you can't even pray. You must have confidence in your prayers, or you will be a prayerless Christian. And without prayer you will be rendered ineffective. The Bible is unambiguous when it comes to masks. You don't have to wear veils and masquerade around in a world of pretend. You have the liberty to be free and not pretend but to be who you really are and grow into the person God wants you to be.

It is so easy to pretend and many are not willing to be unmasked. Others from the depths of their hearts want more than anything else to be accepted. It goes like this: "How are you doing spiritually today?" And we answer, "Fine," when in reality we are in a death struggle for our faith, and we are doing awful. And, to make matters worse, in most churches we are not free to unmask. We are encouraged to wear veils as we are told, "If you are a real Christian, you shouldn't feel that way. If you are a real Christian, you shouldn't have those temptations. If you were a real Christian, you wouldn't have sinned." So we just keep hiding.

Evil, when it is hidden, grows and multiplies; it thrives in darkness. Sin and evil cannot stand exposure to the light. You never see people when they are falling. You always see them after they have hit. Most people that hit have been falling for a long time. Sad to say, they were not able or even encouraged to cry out for help. We have watched some of the best known preachers in the world fall to sexual immorality, and we were left wondering why. Lust precedes adultery—usually for years. Help was near, but the tempted never asked for it because of their mask.

When is the last time you practiced James 5:16? "Confess your faults one to another, and pray one for another, that ye may be healed." I know we all know this verse is in the Bible but how many times have we practiced it? I am not encouraging you to tell everyone or just anyone your business. God sends us accountability partners, those we can trust with our life or our wife. We have the liberty to express our inner selves to them without any fear of rejection.

What would happen in our churches if we just became honest with one another, and we sincerely were concerned and really would pray for one another? I will tell you: Revival would sweep into our churches like a hurricane from the gulf reenergizing us with a fresh anointing to heal our land. God's promise still stands, and there would be a major unmasking;

"If my people, which are called by my name, shall humble themselves, and pray, and seek my face, and turn from their wicked ways; then will I hear from heaven, and will forgive their sin, and will heal their land" (II Chronicles 7:14).

How many of our prayers are veiled prayers? Again you are rarely honest when you pray. Have you ever told God you didn't like the circumstance you were in? Instead we put on a pious tone that sounds like we swallowed a communion cup and we veil our prayers. But that is not what is really in our heart and then we make believe that God doesn't know.

Read the Psalms and see how honest and sincere the psalmists were with God. Psalms 73 is a prime example. The psalmist was confused, bewildered, envious, and almost taken down when he saw the prosperity of the wicked. Then he looked at the problems of his own life and asked the age-old question, "What is the good in being good?" He wondered, "Does it really pay to live right?" So he asked God these questions, and when he entered into the house of God, God of the house gave him the answers.

We have become masters of disguise. Husbands wear their masks when with their wives, and wives wear their masks when around their husbands. (Of course the women wear designer masks.) Pastors are afraid to be transparent around their members, and members will never ask for help because of the fear of what the preacher will think about them. I recently saw a cartoon that illustrates this truth. A little boy is standing up in the couch with drapes pulled back, while the pastor is walking toward the house with in twenty-five feet of the door. The boy turns to yell back in the kitchen to his mother, "Mom the preacher is coming to the door! Is there anything you want me to hide?" If you have to hide something, that should be a good indication that it is wrong.

Pastors should be transparent and never dim the fact that preachers have clay feet. However, I realize ministers cannot allow people to become too close, otherwise they lose their efficiency and effectiveness to minister. It is such a tight rope for a preacher to walk that I like to say, "Preachers should be transparent but not completely see through." But they should always be see through to God. God sees the good, the bad and the ugly.

We sometimes express emotions we do not feel. We tell one another "I love You," simply because we don't have the liberty or the courage to say, "I have a problem and I need to get it straightened out, now." We camouflage our criticisms with complaints. Have you been guilty of meeting a brother in the hallway and saying, "I appreciate you," then turning the corner and thinking to yourself, "What a jerk!"?

We have names for our masks. We call them diplomacy, tact, poise or making a good impression. If we want to get really politically correct, we call them, delicate perception of the right thing to say or do without offending, skill in dealing with people.

But God calls it lying. Churches split over this one thing. People carry bitter feelings for years and never put them on the altar.

Let me ask another question since I am in a question-asking mood. In the last year, have you practiced what Paul taught? "Nevertheless, when it shall turn to the Lord, the veil shall be taken away. Now the Lord is that Spirit: and where the Spirit of the Lord is, there is liberty" (II Corinthians 3:16). We of Pentecostal persuasion have always interpreted this to mean if the Spirit of God is present we have liberty to shout, run, buck and snort and, where available, swing from the chandeliers. Let's look at this in context: Where the Spirit of the Lord is there is liberty to take off the mask (veil) and be honest. If you were living in Old Testament times it would have been hard to take the veil off. Insecurity was just par for the course, and people lived under the bondage of the mask. But when you live with security in Christ, you are fully aware that you are completely accepted by God as much as anyone else. Others won't easily intimidate you, and if you have a problem (which may be in the form of a habit, weakness, or even sin.) you know the Lord is there to help you and not condemn you. You have complete confidence that God has placed you in the Body to be healed. Any healthy body heals itself, and this is by God's design.

Instead of wearing an old, heavy, inconvenient mask, wouldn't it be much easier to take it off when God gives you the opportunity to lift the veil? You can, because God does give you that opportunity everyday. As long as you keep playing the games of religion, you will stay unhealed. You may go to a church service and be inspired and even excited and leave enthusiastic but not healed. Blessings on the outside don't last long, but the blessings on the inside can last for eternity. When God does something on the inside, you will never, never, never be the same again.

Paul says, "And this I pray, that your love may abound yet more and more in knowledge and in all judgment; That ye may approve things that are excellent; that ye may be sincere and without offence till the day of Christ; Being filled with the fruits of righteousness, which are by Jesus Christ, unto the glory and praise of God" (Philippians 1:9).

The word "sincere" in this scripture literally means judged by sunlight or tested as genuine. The word comes from two Latin words, "meaning without wax." The ancient Romans were great lovers of marble statues. A hairline crack would render a priceless statue worthless. If one was trying to hide the cracks, the solution was to rub wax into the cracks. Then the statue was taken into a cool, dim place where no one could tell it wasn't perfect. The only true test of inspection was to take the statue into the sunlight and to let the heat of the sun melt any wax, if the statue was flawed.

You may pretend for years or even a lifetime. No one may know your true identity. But the day of Christ is swiftly approaching, and you will be brought into His glorious light there nothing is hidden and all things are revealed. The solution is to take off the mask right now, repent, and be real. Live without wax and be sincere. Face it. We are all a bunch of cracked pots with imperfections, in desperate need for the healing touch of the Master's hand. We need His grace now. And, don't forget,

He is the Master Potter with the supernatural ability to makes us new. He makes cracked pots into priceless treasures. He gives beauty for ashes.

The Lone Ranger wore a mask to obscure his identity for a good reason. I have yet to discover a legitimate reason to hide the real you. And it makes no difference if you are a Christian or not. Who are the masked men and women who now hold this book in their hands? The title of this chapter is in the past tense, "Who Was That Masked Man?" That is God's ideal plan for your life, to make your mask wear past tense. He knows who you are, how you are, and what you are. He will take your life now and give you a new one. "If the Son therefore shall make you free, ye shall be free indeed" (John 8:36). You don't have to hide under a mask anymore.

He will give you a song in the night and take your tears and turn them into triumphs. He will take your mourning and turn it into laughter. Jesus Christ can heal every broken past, carry every impossible burden, divide every Red sea, walk with you in every fiery furnace, and set you free from every addiction. Christ is the answer. He never fails.

So what are you waiting for? Try Him and ride off into the sunset leaving the devil to ask the question, "Who was that masked man?" He is not masked anymore! Grace has set him free!

CHAPTER SEVEN

MERCY DRAPED IN SKIN

———◆—◆—◆—◆—◆———

Tongue cannot tell, throat cannot sing;
Hands cannot paint, the
tragedy that was enacted at Calvary.
Gather the wail from the icy winds
that howl through the frozen north.
Extract the heart despair of a mother
watching wild beast tear at the throat of her baby.
Capture all the hopeless shrieks of the damned
in the land of shadows and unending doom.
And with all of this at your command,
you will still be unable to paint the
picture which is Calvary!

—Unknown Author

THE CROSS WAS God's answer to our sin. Christ gave His body to be beaten, bruised, and broken on a cruel Roman cross for us. It seems, from my perspective, the farther we trek from that dark, dreary day in time when Jesus died on the cross, the less we understand or even appreciate the depth of sacrifice and the debt that was paid. His broken body should stir our hearts and drive us to our knees.

As often as we gather together we ought to remember His death. For it was neither His miracles nor His mastery over death that saved us. It was not His wonderful life that raised us up from the dunghill. It was His death and His death alone! "And almost all things are by the law purged with blood; and without shedding of blood is no remission" (Hebrews 9:22). Not even His resurrection was the saving factor of our salvation. The resurrection gave validly to the Cross. If Jesus had not been resurrected, then the Cross would have been meaningless. But thanks be unto God, Jesus was resurrected and the Cross is the redemptive power of Christ!

The Old Testament altars represent the New Testament Cross. God made comprehensible to those ancient Jews that at those altars of Israel the severity must not be hidden from the human sight of men. They say one could smell those altars a mile away. Death was there. Blood was there. Raw flesh was there. The innocent were dying for the guilty, and God wanted every man to see that, because those altars were only a picture of the world's greatest coming event, Calvary. God states in the book of Deuteronomy, "Thou shalt not plant thee a grove of any trees near unto the altar of the LORD thy God, which thou shalt make thee. Neither shalt thou set thee up any image; which the LORD thy God hateth" (Deuteronomy 16:21–22).

The heathen in their attempt to seek their gods also built altars and shed blood. The devil will always counterfeit the true and the real. However, the heathen in their endeavor to lessen the brutality of death and to mask the awful smell of blood, planted groves, gardens, and placed beautiful images around their altars. The smell of blood was too repulsive to them. But God said don't even think about putting trees in bloom or budding roses around my altars. Leave the altar naked because men must see the severity of it all.

Our generation has become so politically correct, and our churches have become so seeker friendly that we stand poised on the edge of fear everyday that we are going to offend someone. Whole denominations have removed any mention of blood, and many have removed any visible sign of the cross. It has been stated that the Cross is too offensive. But really nothing is new under the sun. The devil has fought the message of the blood and the Cross from the very beginning.

G. Campbell Morgan, a preacher who was born one hundred years before my birth, said, "There are people who look upon the Cross of Christ as vulgar. We agree it is the most vulgar object in the history of the world. But whose is the vulgarity? Not that of God's Son who gave His blood to wash away our sin."

It is the vulgarity of our sin that nailed Him to the Cross. It is the vulgarity of the sin of those who deny the necessity of the Cross and make sin such a light thing. No one can look at the cross and make light of sin. If you want to see God's judgment on sin then look at the Cross. You will see God's very Best hanging in a bloody mess and, as the prophet Isaiah wrote, "He was even unrecognizable as a man."

You will not find any lilac garden around the Cross, no perfume sprinkled on it or tulip path leading up to it. Only blood and only death. Calvary is not a flashy spectacle; it is a bloody horror. God's only begotten Son died there. Look at Him as He walks up those cobblestone streets of the old city of Jerusalem with a crown of thorns on His head and a Roman cross on His back, headed for an outlaw's grave. There was nothing beautiful about this at all. Execution by Cross was the most gruesome and horrible death men ever died.

Again God said, "Tear down every tree, cut down every flower, and without any sentiment destroy every trace of decoration, altars of incense, imitation, and corruption on the Cross." God would that all men were saved. That is why He sent His Son. He wants to save all men, but the church must not think that lowering the standard to cater to the lust of the world will result in their acceptance. God only accepts the divine sacrifice of the old rugged Cross.

This truth can be illustrated by Jesus's parable of the prodigal son. If that son had been given a continuous supply of ice cream and cake, he would have never left the hog pen. As long as we sugarcoat the message of the Cross sinners will never leave the hog pen of the world. They must see the depravity of sin and they can only see how vile sin is by looking at the Cross.

May God help the Church to tear away the groves, the images, decorations, and tapestries from around the Cross that the world might see God's only plan for redemption. Because we have corrupted the pattern of the Cross, people are brought in to the church under a false pretense. We have removed the Cross or at least sweet scented the path that leads up to it, until the liar, the adulterer, the gambler, and the brewery owner can sit down in the Church of Jesus Christ and feel no guilt or condemnation. The carnal nature on its way to hell can be at ease in the Church.

But the Cross planted in the Church in its naked splendor tells everyone God hates sin, and if a man comes to Jesus, he must be willing to give up his sin.

Jesus was not tied to the cross. He was nailed to it. When Christ was crucified, the Cross stood for all that was vile, low, and degrading. Yet the Apostles never dimmed or hid the fact that Jesus, whom they boldly preached as the only Savior of the world, had been hung on a cross and crucified. Paul wrote "For the preaching of the cross is to them that perish foolishness; but unto us which are saved it is the power of God" (I Corinthians 1:18).

What are we telling men? Are we just bringing them in the church with just a handshake, or are we bringing them in with the naked splendor of the Cross of Christ? The worst thing man has ever done *to* man became the best thing ever done *for* man. The worst thing man has ever done was to hang Jesus on a tree, and nail the Son of God to the Cross. And as He hung there in lonely, naked shame with a crown of thorns on His head, one could see His body had been beaten to look almost like hamburger meat. He was dying for the sins of humanity. This was by far the best thing ever done for man.

It is almost impossible for our western minds to fully comprehend the Cross. Some Roman coins were inscribed with a donkey hanging on a cross. This is what the Roman world thought of anyone who hung on a cross and of anyone who worshiped a man that died on a cross. The Church must remember the Cross as a terrible thing.

I am not suggesting it is a sin to wear a cross around one's neck. However, God never intended for us to make the cross just a cheap piece of costume jewelry. People who don't live for God have found it fashionable to wear a gold cross or to sprinkle the cross with diamonds and wear it as a dinner necklace or earrings.

The Cross is not a good luck piece like a rabbit's foot or four leaf clover. It was the instrument of death that the Romans used to put the most wicked criminals to demise. It was the equivalent of the hangman's gallows or the electric chair. God chose the Cross as the means to bleed out the Son of God for the sins of this planet.

Paul said to the Corinthian Church, "For I determined not to know any thing among you, save Jesus Christ, and him crucified" (I Corinthians 2:2). The city of Corinth was, to say the least, one of the ancient world's most immoral and depraved cities. Prostitution and perversion were a way of life. God told Paul to take the gospel there and preach the truth of Jesus Christ. Paul stood there with his instructions, figuring how he would do that. I believe he resurrected that Cross, planted it in the streets of Corinth.

He preached Jesus and Him crucified and with the long piercing thorns from Judea stabbed into His brow. With nail prints in His hands and feet, His back flayed open, with spit on His face and blood matted in His hair. And he said to those Corinthians, "The Romans or the Jews didn't kill Jesus. Your sin nailed Him to that Cross!"

He never planted a tree or sowed rose bush around the Cross. He simply said, "You nailed Him to the Cross, and you need to see the shame of it and feel the guilt." If an individual is to know the joy, peace and deliverance that only the blood of Jesus can bring, then that individual must confess that he was there. This makes it a highly personal matter; it was his sin that nailed Christ to the Cross.

The biggest misconception Jews ever made was to think Christ was paying the penalty for His own sin. What fools! He had no sin. They took Him in their evil hands and thrashed Him, spat on Him, tore the beard from His face, cursed Him, humiliated Him, profaned Him and degraded Him to the lowest level. Yet He opened not His mouth but went as a sheep to the slaughter. It was our transgressions for which He suffered not His. He had none: "But he was wounded for our transgressions, he was bruised for our iniquities: the chastisement of our peace was upon him; and with his stripes we are healed" (Isaiah53:5).

The Cross is stamped on almost each and every page of the New Testament. The Epistles were actually written before the Gospels. They tell us little about the life of Jesus, but they center in on His death and His resurrection.

In the Gospels we learn about the life of Jesus. God pulls back the curtain, and we catch a short glimpse of Christ's earthly life. Some chapters deal with an entire year in His life.

But, when all four writers approach the eternal Cross and the fact of His death, the pace slows down. The final hours of Jesus' life are written in detail, in all four gospels. This breaks from the trend of secular authors such as William Manchester who wrote *One Brief Shining Moment* about the life of John F. Kennedy. It is a 280 page book and only ten pages are dedicated to his death.

The death of Jesus is our salvation. It is…

The foundation of our joy.

The anchor of our faith.

The refuge of our hope.

I will cling to the old rugged cross because…

### 1.	The Cross is a Condemnation.

Before we can accept the deliverance of the Cross we must first accept it's Condemnation.

### 2.	The Cross is a Reconciliation.

This is the paradox of the Cross. The Cross that condemns us is the same Cross that reconciles us back to God.

### 3.	The Cross is a Separation.

It separates us from the world and separates unto God. It is so much more than a theological and religious symbol.

### 4.	The Cross is a Celebration.

It is God's final victory over evil. His victory is our victory, and, not only will we celebrate it in eternity but we celebrate now in time.

Always keep in mind that the Old Testament altar is a shadow of the New Testament Cross. God said to the Israelites In Exodus,

> An altar of earth thou shalt make unto me, and shalt sac-
> rifice thereon thy burnt offerings, and thy peace offerings,
> thy sheep, and thine oxen: in all places where I record my

name I will come unto thee, and I will bless thee. And if
thou wilt make me an altar of stone, thou shalt not build
it of hewn stone: for if thou lift up thy tool upon it, thou
hast polluted it (Exodus 20:24–25).

This altar of dirt was to give a type of the Cross as God's work
unaided by the human touch of man. Everything man has ever touched
he has messed up. So God said, if any stone was used, it was to be an
un-hewn stone. No hand should touch it, or it would be polluted.
Again—it cannot be emphasized enough—the Cross is God's work,
single-handedly done; without question, man had nothing to do with it.
It is all about what God did, not what man has done. The human touch
pollutes the Cross. Plant one tree, pour one drop of perfume, set one vase
of flowers by it, and you have polluted it.

On the night of the Passover, God's acting representative for deliverance was blood. Even the agent of sprinkling was to be untouched
by human hands. The Israelites were commanded to use the hyssop.
This is what is wrong with religion. Religion cannot save you. It is a
sham, a farce, a fake. Because religion is man's attempt to reach God.
But salvation is not about man reaching God. You see, this is the whole
problem: Man cannot reach God any more than a cowboy can lasso the
North Star. God is too high and too holy. He is too right and too righteous. It would be like a man trying to jump over the Grand Canyon.
No long jumper who ever lived could come close. And there has never
been a man able to reach God through religion. You can't do it through
sacraments, baptism, rosary beads, confessional booths, good works,
giving money or even giving your body to be burned. Our man-made
attempts to reach God are as filthy rags in God's sight. Man cannot reach
God, and God knows it, so He sent His Son Jesus Christ. He was born
of a virgin, lived, died and was resurrected. And He lives forevermore.
You can't be God, but God became man to set you free from sin and
every entanglement.

THERE WAS ONLY ONE PERFECT MAN WHO EVER LIVED
THE REST OF US HAVE TO SWIM

Christianity is not a principle, not a policy, not a political stance, but a Person. Jesus is not a movement, but He is the Messiah. He is not a creed, but He is the Christ. He is the only hope of salvation. We can't add one thing to God's plan of salvation. And to try is to pollute it. Jesus is the perfect sacrifice. Perfection is the least that God will accept. Everything on this sinful planet is defective except Jesus. So trust Him and His finished work on the Cross.

There is a story of the kindly priest who was making the rounds in the hospital. He came to a ward where death hovered near an elderly saint. For more than sixty years, she had been on a pilgrimage to the city where there is no night.

"Good morning," he said graciously, "I have come to grant you forgiveness."

"I'm sorry," she answered. "I do not understand what you mean."

"I have come to forgive your sins," he explained.

"May I see your hands?" she questioned.

Somewhat puzzled he held out his hands.

"You cannot do it," she exclaimed earnestly "The One who forgives my sins has nail-pierced hands."

"He is not the one who can," says the doubter. "He is the only one who can," says the delivered. Jesus Christ is mercy draped in skin. He is grace garbed in flesh. Oh, what a Savior!

CHAPTER EIGHT

THE COLOR OF REDEMPTION

———————

CONTRARY TO COMMON perception, the color of redemption is not red. Red is the color of the blood of Jesus, which is the divine agency that brings redemption. The color of redemption is the color of pearl. Not red, but white. As a matter of fact, God even uses the color red as the color of sin. "Come now, and let us reason together, saith the LORD: though your sins be as scarlet, they shall be as white as snow; though they be red like crimson, they shall be as wool" (Isaiah 1:18). Scarlet is red and the wool of sheep is white. In the last book of the Bible, there is a stirring picture of redeemed saints that are described as having their garments made white by the blood of the Lamb. "And I said unto him, Sir, thou knowest. And he said to me, These are they which came out of great tribulation, and have washed their robes, and made them white in the blood of the Lamb" (Revelation 7:14).

If you are more than a casual reader of the Bible, it doesn't take you long to realize God uses types, shadows, allegories, and parables to artic-ulate timeless truths. Leprosy is a deadly acute disease that slowly kills the victim. It first isolates. The nature of the disease mandates the afflicted be placed in a leper colony, away and out of sight of the mainstream society. Then it disfigures and deforms the body in a slow agonizing process leading to paralysis and blindness. And it eventually takes the person's life. Leprosy is a type for sin. But on occasion, if leprosy was healed, the leper was commanded to go to the priest and be declared clean. "Then the priest shall consider: and, behold, [if] the leprosy have covered all his flesh, he shall pronounce [him] clean [that hath] the plague: it is all turned white: he [is] clean," (Leviticus 13:13).

We are born with the severe infection of sin that isolated us from God. From the day we were born, sin began its dastardly exertion to deform us. We were made in the image of God, but sin changes that appearance. In time, sin paralyzes unbelievers and blinds them to the truth that the Gospel came to bring. Ultimately, the soul is swept away in a maelstrom of iniquity, for the wages of sin is still death. But Jesus came to cleanse the leper physically and spiritually! "And, behold, there came a leper and worshipped him, saying, Lord, if thou wilt, thou canst make me clean. And Jesus put forth [his] hand, and touched him, saying, I will; be thou clean. And immediately his leprosy was cleansed" (Matthew 8:2–3). At the point of Christ's contact we are clean and declared white as snow. Again, white is the color of redemption!

Jesus gives a parable in Matthew 13:45–46, "Again, the kingdom of heaven is like unto a merchant man, seeking goodly pearls: Who, when he had found one pearl of great price, went and sold all that he had, and bought it." Of all the parables Jesus taught, the parable of the "Pearl of Great Price" is by far (to me) the most exceptional gem of the example of God's astonishing grace or our undeserved redemption. Unmerited salvation is only made possible because of Jesus.

You could take a cup—be it gold, silver or clay—and pass it down the line to every human being on the face of the earth, which has been scientifically calculated to have over six billion people. If you stood six billion people heel to toe, the line would stretch from earth to the moon and back five times. (That's one line I wouldn't want to stand in).

Ask all six billion to put their goodness and righteousness in the cup as it passed by.

When it finally got all the way to the last person, how full do you think the cup would be?

Let me tell you: It would be empty.

The "Pearl of Great Price" is not Jesus but we, the Church. We didn't find Jesus. He found us. He purchased us because we couldn't purchase Him or His salvation. Before we were saved we were spiritually bankrupt. Basically, we were beggars, and beggars have no money. Besides, Jesus is not for sale. He is a free gift; so, it is clear in the parable Jesus is the merchant and we are the pearl.

The formation of a pearl is extremely fascinating: Into the oyster comes a piece of foreign matter—accurately spoken, a bit of irritant like a grain of sand, grime, or grit. It wounds the oyster in its side and seats itself inside the mussel. Then the oyster reacts to the wound by secreting a substance called "nacre." The oyster oozes out this liquid that coats the grain of sand and then it hardens around it. The oyster keeps doing this over and over until the grit no longer causes pain. Something that started out being painful turned into something very beautiful and valuable. Beauty is made out of ugly, and something glorious is made out of something hurtful.

HOW THE PEARL WAS WROUGHT

There are four incredible parallels here. The Church has gone from...

Grit to Glory: We were an impurity or some foreign object. Don't take offense to this but we were just a filthy piece of dirt and we wounded Him. We crucified the Lord of glory in our stupidity, pride, and ignorance. From the wounded side of our dear Redeemer poured forth not only blood and water but also love and mercy. He took that which wounded

Him, that which was dirty, ugly, and impure and laid upon it a beauty that was not its own. Jesus took our life that was worthless and made us a precious jewel, something beautiful and something made of value.

Depths to Heights: A precious pearl is lying down in the depths of the ocean floor. One day a diver comes and discovers it. That diver extracts it and then brings it to the surface. This pearl is discovered, and, instead of being taken to the market, it is thought too valuable to sell. It is rushed to the King's palace. It's so beautiful—this pearl of great price—that it is fit for one thing and one thing only. The common man is undeserving of it. But it belongs to the diadem of the King, to rest high upon the tiara of the King. The pearl has gone from the mega-depths of the mire of the ocean to the magnificent heights of the crown of the King.

Darkness to Light: What could be darker than the inside of an oyster on the bottom of the ocean? Only one thing I can think of—the soul of an unsaved individual. The darkness of sin is darker than anything humanly conceived. Jesus came into the world to bring the light of His presence into the darkness of this world. He is the light and in Him is no darkness. He brought us out of darkness into His marvelous light. All other gems reflect light. This is what brings luster to the jewel. The pearl not only reflects light, it also absorbs light. We not only reflect the light of Jesus, we also absorb the light and the light becomes our source of life. We have gone from the deepest, darkest state we could ever envision to the brightest light we could ever believe.

Start to Finish: Forming a pearl is a lengthy procedure that takes a lot of time and effort for the oyster to accomplish. It can take up to two years to complete the process. The costliest of all pearls are the ones without blemish. "That he might sanctify and cleanse it with the washing of water by the word, That he might present it to himself a glorious church, not having spot, or wrinkle, or any such thing; but that it should be holy and without blemish" (Ephesians 5:26). No matter how difficult the task or how lengthy the process Jesus will finish the work He has begun. "Being confident of this very thing, that he which hath begun a good work in you will perform [it] until the day of Jesus Christ" (Philippians 1:6).

That is how the pearl was wrought. Now let's see how the pearl was sought.

HOW THE PEARL WAS SOUGHT

The merchant was seeking goodly pearls. This merchant is a picture of the Lord Jesus Christ. The mission of Jesus is reflected in His statement, "For the Son of man is come to seek and to save that which was lost" (Luke 19:10). If you sought the Lord, it is because He first sought you. After Adam sinned, Adam didn't run through the garden saying, "God, where are you?" We learn in Genesis 3:9 that God went looking for Adam: "And the LORD God called unto Adam, and said unto him, Where [art] thou?" From that day until this God has been seeking man.

In his first chapter Ezekiel said he saw what he called "A wheel in the middle of a wheel." There are more heavenly implications there than I could ever explain. However, I am left with the overwhelming feeling, after reading about Ezekiel's wheel in the middle of a wheel, that God has a plan. Everything on which everything is revolving is revolving around God. Everything, past, present and future, is revolving around Jesus Christ. He is not just a man of history, but He's the center, the focal point, the wheel in the middle of a wheel. All the wars, all the people who have ever been born, all the civilizations that have ever risen are wrapped around one central hub, Christ Jesus, God's Son. This may come as a shock, but you are not the center of the universe. What is at the center of the whole universe is the dynamic force of an Almighty God. He is like a gyrator. Everything revolves and rotates around Him.

What are atoms? Atoms are the basic building blocks of matter that make up everyday objects. A desk, a car, even you are made up of atoms. Atoms are the smallest unit of matter. Scientists so far have found 112 different kinds of atoms. Everything in the world is made of different combinations of these atoms. The atom is the smallest part of an element that still has all properties of that element. Its nucleus consists of protons and neutrons and is surrounded by orbiting electrons. The orbiting electrons pull all matter together.

Like an atom, Jesus (who, by the way, was the Creator of the atom) is at the center of everything and everything orbits and is spinning around Him. Everything is held in and together by the magnetism of the power of His presence. Just as there is a geographical pull in the center of the earth, Jesus pulls everything to Himself.

Have you ever owned a gyroscope? What is a gyroscope? It is a wheel in the middle of a wheel. It pulls everything to the center, and that is why it can be balanced on a pencil. Everything is drawn to the center giving it perfect balance. This gives reason to what Jesus said: "And I, if I be lifted up from the earth, will draw all [men] unto me" (John 12:32). When Jesus is at the center of your life, He gives your life perfect balance. I didn't say your life would be perfect; but God is perfect, and when He is at the center of your life, like a compass He keeps you focused in the storm.

He sought you, and if you are a Christian, you are one only because He drew you by His Spirit. "No man can come to me, except the Father which hath sent me draw him: and I will raise him up at the last day" (John 6:44). You didn't wake up one day and decide to turn over a new leaf. You were sought and you were drawn. "Well, I found Jesus!" No, you didn't. He found you. Jesus was never lost. You were. You were the one that was on the bottom of sin's ocean. Pardon me please, but you didn't know your head from a hole in the ground (spiritually speaking). You were the one who was bound by sin and captive of the devil. So it is not your seeking Him; it is Him seeking you. It is not Jesus's working into your plan but it is your working into His plan.

A preacher went to an insane asylum to preach the Gospel to the mentally impaired. The residents were all gathered in the lobby looking at one another in total incomprehension. The preacher stood behind a makeshift pulpit and read from the book of Genesis the story of the creation of man. After he had so purposely read his text, he proceeded to preach his finely tuned homiletic sermon on the subject, "God's purpose for man." He began with a question: "Do you know why we are here?" There was no response; it was as quiet as a cemetery. It kind of irritated the preacher because he was very response oriented. So he asked the question again, expecting a little retort, "Do you know why we are here?" Suddenly, an old gentleman stood up near the back and said, "Preacher, I think we are all here because we ain't all there."

Let me ask you; do you know why we are here? Take it, you may not be all there, but you are in the kingdom because Jesus sought you. In the sacred precincts of eternity God the Father signed a warrant for your arrest. The Spirit of God was dispatched to bring you in, and He found you. The God of the universe drew you by His Holy Spirit. He found you when you were as lost as a goose in a hailstorm going north for the winter. He took you when no one else would have you. He called your name when you didn't even know His.

In the pitch black of your midnight experience He shined His ever-loving, everlasting light of grace into your pitiful excuse for human existence. And like a ten million pound magnet He jerked you up out of the pit you were in. He then looked at the devil and said, "That will be enough of that because they belong to me!" You are only here because He loves you, sought you, and drew you unto Himself.

A deep-sea diver who on the bottom of the ocean floor found (submerged in the sand) a bottle with a cork in it. He brought it up to the surface. He opened it, and on the inside was a Gospel track with a scripture explaining how much God loved him. He was spiritually stirred in his soul so much that he bowed his head in repentance. He said to the Lord, "God, if you love me enough to follow me to the bottom of the ocean, I will give my heart to you!" Listen, friend. God will follow you to the ends of the earth saying, "I love you, I seek you, and I want you!"

That is how the pearl was sought. Now let's look at how the pearl is bought.

HOW THE PEARL WAS BOUGHT

In the parable that Jesus taught, who bought the pearl? The merchant did. Who does the merchant represent? That is easy—Jesus Christ. Christ bought the Church with His blood: "For ye are bought with a price" (I Corinthians 6:20). Jesus was the price, and Jesus was the buyer.

Do you remember what happened in the garden of Gethsemane on that memorable night of betrayal? It is recorded: "And he went a little further, and fell on his face, and prayed, saying, O my Father, if it be possible, let this cup pass from me: nevertheless not as I will, but as thou [wilt]" (Matthew 26:39).

What was the cup? It was not physical death Jesus wrestled with. He is the resurrection, and He knew it. He is trapped in a pang of pain over a cup that was invisible to the human eye. If you had been standing on the edge of the garden with the moonbeams floating through the foliage, you could not have seen the cup. He looks through the abyss of despair and sees a cup. The power of evil which He had intentionally undertaken to annihilate appeared so malignant and mighty, the hell of sin so deep, black, and thick, the peril of man so looming and appalling, and the work of redemption so difficult to accomplish, that His soul was troubled, and, as the Gospel of Mark records, "He was sore amazed and to be very heavy" (Mark 14:33). His spirit fainted within Him.

When His hour came and the weight of our sins was upon Him, the cup seemed as if it were greater than He ever imagined it to be. His entire nervous system tried violently to shut down. He was trodden to the earth by sin's mass of malignancy. His blood was mingled with His sweat. He cried out for another way, but there was no other way.

Jesus holds a cup in His hands, the same hands that dug man out of the red dirt of Eden and orchestrated the DNA blue print of every human being that one day would be, and designed the course of the celestial universe. The same hands that traced out every river, buried every ocean, stood up every mountain, and fashioned every animal and creeping thing from an elephant to a chigger, now holds a cup. His disciples all slept on a leafy garden carpet as He prayed and watched.

He watches a deranged psycho butcher a little girl just to get a sexual thrill. And degradation and abomination settle to the bottom of the cup. He watches as a woman of the night sells her body like a cheap piece of meat at the market just to supply the money for one more high of methamphetamine. And addiction reaches the cup. He watches as a man breaks the marital commitment he made to God and his wife as he goes home with a mistress and commits adultery. And unfaithfulness is in the cup.

I want you to imagine again that line of six billion people. Then I want you to add to that all who ever lived or all who will ever live and imagine, as that cup passes, everyone puts his and her sin into it. They put their lying, lust, hatred, rape murder, theft, arson, and perversion into the cup. They put in every evil exploit born out of the black hardened heart of human hell. Every blotch of depravity and soil of decadence sinks like thick, black sludge to the bottom of the cup.

In Gethsemane, Jesus put the cup to His lips and drank every drop. The iniquity of us all was laid upon Him, and He was willing. Then He went to Calvary and gave His blood as full payment for our sin. He bought the pearl!

Jesus, who was infinite, suffered for a finite period of time. You are finite, and, if it weren't for Him, you would have suffered for an infinite amount of time. All of history past, present, and future were compressed upon Jesus. He literally died a billion deaths. No man ever suffered like Jesus. His capacity for suffering was greater than anyone else's.

A mothers dies, leaving a three-year-old daughter and a thirty-three-year-old husband. The daughter will suffer and cry but soon will go back to playing with her dolls. The husband will suffer probably for the rest of his life. She can suffer as a little girl, but he will suffer as a man. He has a deeper capacity for suffering.

No one had a deeper capacity of suffering for sorrow, as did Christ. He was known as a man of sorrows. The sin and shame of the whole world was put upon Him. The centuries were compressed upon Him. That is why you cannot suffer anything that He has not already felt. "For we have not an high priest which cannot be touched with the feeling of our infirmities; but was in all points tempted like as [we are, yet] without sin" (Hebrews 4:15).

That scripture is saying He can be touched with the feeling of all our infirmities because He is not an earthly high priest. He is the high priest that came from heaven, and we wounded Him. The thing that wounded Him He has made into something beautiful, something of value. The Church is the Pearl of Great Price. Jesus sold everything He had to buy it. When He is finished with the pearl, He will come and receive it unto Himself.

CHAPTER NINE

FROM THE MIRE TO THE CHOIR

IT TOOK A bloody war to legally abolish slavery in our nation. But the wheels were set in motion many years before this was a reality. The great emancipator Abraham Lincoln was stirred in his spirit when, as a young man, he visited New Orleans, Louisiana. He had what he called a ghastly experience when he saw the inhumanity of how the black people were treated. The pictures of whole families being sold—some as a unit, some individually—never left his mind. The pain, the disappointment, the agony, the discrimination, and the immorality of the institution of slavery made him sick to his stomach and haunted him in his sleep.

Long after this horrible experience on New Years Day, 1863, the President of the United States signed into law *The Emancipation Proclamation*. This order gave autonomy to all slaves in the rebel states. Even though it was publicly avowed on that day, it wasn't until December 18, 1865, that the constitution made emancipation a reality. The Thirteenth Amendment officially abolished slavery in the United States of America.

THERE WAS ONLY ONE PERFECT MAN WHO EVER LIVED
THE REST OF US HAVE TO SWIM

After the great Civil War was ended and the southern slave was freed, a strange incongruity occurred that even Abraham Lincoln had not even imagined. Though the slaves were free, many never claimed this new freedom, and a majority of them stayed on the plantations and farms as slaves. Even though they technically were free, they continued their lives as though they were never emancipated, as though the war had never been fought.

History bears it out that many ex-slaves throughout the Reconstruction Period lived in effect the same as they lived before their emancipation. Every slave could repeat authentically what one Alabama slave said when asked what he thought of Abraham Lincoln his great emancipator. "I don't know nothing about Abraham Lincoln," he replied, "'Cept they say he set us free. And I know nothing about that neither." What a tragedy! Thousands of men gave the ultimate sacrifice. The President in like manner had his life taken from him in Ford's theater just a few days after the war was ended. The Thirteenth Amendment had been signed into law. But the ex-slaves, though they were legally free, still had a slave's mentality.

Remember the ex-slaves that came out of Egypt? They vacated their Egyptian premises in one night, but it took forty years to extract Egypt out of them. The slave mentality is so hard to penetrate. We were all slaves to sin and Satan from our birth. Whole families and each individual were born into slavery. We were captive to an evil taskmaster that treated us with a wicked disdain. Dignity, respect, and common courtesy were not an everyday luxury. We were treated like the slaves we were.

But one day our Great Emancipator, Jesus Christ, came and with His blood bought us off the auction block of sin and freed us for time and eternity. We are free indeed! But here is where the great problem lies. Though we are legally and spiritually free, many still live like a slave with a slave's mentality. The devil has taken on the philosophy of the old southern slave masters: "Keep them ignorant, and you will keep them in the fields."

If the devil can keep us ignorant of God's grace then, even though we are technically free, we will still be in bondage. Sad to say, many Christians are. There are many Christians who live under a constant cloud of condemnation. The are condemned because of weak prayer lives, broken fasts, lack of Bible reading or a failure to witness their faith to others twenty-four hours a day. These spiritual endeavors are great, and we should be involved in the Lord's work. Praying and being diligent in the Word are not only a necessity but also an imperative for our spiritual growth and survival.

However, if you can show me that these activities are the foundation for my salvation, then I will personally live under that cloud with you. The Bible says, "For by grace are ye saved through faith; and that not of yourselves: it is the gift of God: Not of works, lest any man should boast" (Ephesians 2:8–9).

Here is the deal: You and I could never pray enough, read the Bible enough or witness to enough people to ever buy or negotiate an arrangement to get us into heaven. It is not by works of righteousness but by God's amazing grace that looked beyond our faults and saw our needs. And, besides that, after we have done the very best we can do, the Bible still calls us unprofitable servants.

Now this may be tough; so if you can't stand the heat, you had better get out of the kitchen. If you only go to church out of form or habit, then this should be a red flag to your spiritual experience. You may not be saved. If you are a Christian and you only pray so you won't feel condemned or you only read the Bible because you feel in some way this will appease the wrath of God, then you have the same dark view of God that the witch doctor in Africa has.

God's wrath was appeased at Calvary!

> At Calvary God smote His own Son
> At Calvary Christ was wounded for our transgressions
> At Calvary Christ was bruised for our iniquity
> At Calvary the chastisement of our peace was upon Him.

84

By His stripes we are healed, and it all came from Calvary! At Calvary all condemnation is lifted, the devil is defeated, the death sentence is revoked, sin is forgiven, full pardon is given, the fires of the Law are extinguished, and God's judgment is met perfectly. Calvary is more than just a place; it is the crossroad of humanity, and God's full purpose was accomplished at Calvary.

Condemnation is so much different than conviction. Condemnation says, "You fouled up because you are good for nothing, so go away, you miserable failure." Conviction says, "I love you, and you didn't do right; but, come here and draw near to me and let me forgive you. Now go and sin no more." The devil lives to condemn you, but the devil lost his right at the Cross. Only God has the right to convict you. God is not trying to push you out the door. He is trying to draw you to an altar. A slave lives under condemnation and the feeling of no self-worth. We are not slaves but sons. "There is therefore now no condemnation to them which are in Christ Jesus, who walk not after the flesh, but after the Spirit. For the law of the Spirit of life in Christ Jesus hath made me free from the law of sin and death (Romans 8:1–2). Christ has made us free!

I heard of a preacher of the early twentieth century who said that when he was twelve years old he had killed one of the family geese by throwing a stone and hitting it squarely on the head. Figuring his parents wouldn't notice that one of the twenty-four birds was missing, he buried the dead fowl. But that evening his sister called him aside and said, "I saw what you did. If you don't offer to do the dishes tonight, I'll tell Mother." The next morning she gave him the same warning. All that day and the next the frightened boy felt bound to do the dishes. The following morning, however, he surprised his sister by telling her it was her turn. When she quietly reminded him of what she could do, he replied, "I've already told Mother, and she has forgiven me. Now you do the dishes. Thank God I'm free again!" And he ran out the door praising God.

Christ's mission to this revolving sphere was not to bring parole to the occupants but to employ the full weight of His divine judicial powers to pardon us from sin. He alone has this authority, and He alone has the wisdom to wield this magnitude of responsibility.

The power of pardon is incredible just within the United States. It makes no difference what the crime may have been. Hypothetically, a man could have shot the president's wife, killed the Vice-President, robbed the US. Treasury, burned down the U.S. Capital, blown up the Pentagon, and sold every nuclear ballistic missile we have to terrorists. And all the President has to do is sign a pardon, and that individual is a free man.

Those who have been Pardoned by the President have the rights that every other American citizen has. There will be no discrimination. They can vote, own guns, and buy land. This is the power of an earthly pardon. It is just as though they never committed the crime, and it will never be brought up again. There is no condemnation. They have been set free!

The story is told of a convict who had been in prison for many years. Finally he received a pardon from the king. When the time came for him to be released, he walked boldly to the prison gate and said with confidence, "Me and the king say you have to open the doors and set me free." He then produced the papers signed by the ruler.

The devil may have had you bound for years, and you are guilty of every sin that you have been accused of. But King Jesus signed your pardon. It has been signed, sealed, and delivered in blood. You have been justified—just as though you have never sinned.

The power of God's pardon is so much more far reaching than any earthly pardon signed by a mortal magistrate. Grace is greater than sin. "Moreover the law entered, that the offence might abound. But where sin abounded, grace did much more abound" (Romans 5:20).

There is no doubt, sin is a prevailing force, and if it is left unchecked, it will rule and dominate you. Great men such as Alexander could conquer nations and their known world, but they could not conquer sin. Sin has defeated the strongest of the strong. It has turned the loveliest into the ugliest. It has taken the most brilliant minds and turned them into babbling idiots. This power is the...

THERE WAS ONLY ONE PERFECT MAN WHO EVER LIVED THE REST OF US HAVE TO SWIM

Control of sin

Ability of sin

Nature of sin.

Sin is the author of every tragedy. It is the root of every sickness, and the origin of every disease. It is the cause of every death. Sin has dug every grave, fashioned every casket, stitched every shroud, and planted every tombstone. "Wherefore, as by one man sin entered into the world, and death by sin; and so death passed upon all men, for that all have sinned" (Romans 5:12). The Bible also says, "For the wages of sin is death" (Romans 6:23). Now, if it stopped right there, then this verse wouldn't be called the good news because that is bad news. But, the rest of that scripture in Romans 6:23 says, "but the gift of God is eternal life through Jesus Christ our Lord."

Many people are overwhelmed by desolation, despondency, dejection, and depression because they feel much like a mouse caught in a well-laden trap. They believe the star of hope has set behind the hill of despair, never to rise again. They are convinced the courts of God's mercy have adjourned for time and eternity. They feel stranded on the road of life at the point of no return. But that is a lie. As long as you have breath, hope is on the horizon. Jesus Christ is the Star of Hope, the Judge of the Universe, and the Road of Life. Forgiveness is only a prayer away.

In my estimation there is no better example of grace than that of the penitent thief that all four gospels mention. Never did a case look more hopeless. He was a wicked man. He never lived for God—not even for one minute in his lifetime. He was a dying man who was nailed to a Roman cross never to come down alive. There were only minutes between him and eternity. His grave had already been dug. Hell was just a few short breaths away, so his case looked too far-gone, past recovery and a lost cause for infinity.

But he came in contact with Christ! He was caught just short of too late. He cried out for mercy and said to Jesus, "Lord, remember me when thou comest into thy kingdom" (Luke 23:42). In essence he was saying, "Lord (the Messiah) I believe you are who you say you are."

Suddenly, a new optimism burst forth in his soul when Jesus said unto him, "Verily I say unto thee, today shalt thou be with me in paradise" (Luke 23:43). As quick as you can blink an eye, this thief was completely forgiven, freely justified, instantly sanctified, raised from the gates of hell, and given a title to a prime piece of real estate in a place called paradise. For where sin did abound the grace of God did much more abound.

It matters not what sin you have committed or how hopeless you may feel. Christ never met a sin that He could not conquer, for He is mighty to save. His grace will save, sanctify, satisfy, and seal you unto the day of redemption. His grace will

> Cure,
> Cleanse,
> Change,
> Consecrate,
> and clothe

you in robes of righteousness, all for His namesake. God's grace will cover your sins, blot out your iniquities, strengthen your weakness, and one day sweep you in a golden chariot beyond the farthest star through the gates of pearl.

Jesus Christ was grace in the flesh, and He never met a case He could not cure. Every time He dealt with depraved humanity it was with grace. It came through His words; it came through His actions, and it even came through His clothes. "For the law was given by Moses, but grace and truth came by Jesus Christ" (John 1:17). He dealt with his disciples in grace, forgave Peter at the very moment of his denial, prayed forgiveness on His murderers, called Judas a friend, promised paradise to a dying thief, met Saul on his furious road, and has for two millenniums cried, "If any man thirst, let him come unto me, and drink" (John 7:37).

You may be like Lazarus—dead, buried, and beyond hope—but, as long as there is a living God and a resurrecting Savior, grace is available. I will tell you what grace will do: God's grace will kick down the door, jam hell into the corner, slap the devil aside, roll out the red carpet, and say, "Though your sins be as scarlet, they shall be as white as snow" (Isaiah 1:18).

God's grace is invincible, and there is no power on earth or under the earth that can impede it. Sin cannot stop it. Darkness cannot quench it, and hell cannot prevail against it. You can hit God's grace, slap it, spit upon it, crown it with thorns, strip it naked, drive nails into its hands and into its feet, and it will still look down at you and say, "Father, forgive them, for they know not what they do."

In the history of the great nation many centuries ago, England had a king that since then has become very famous, not for great conquests or military strategy, but for his immoral, adulterous lifestyle. His name is King Henry the VIII. He established the Church of England because the Catholic Church forbade him to remarry. He not only remarried once, he remarried six times.

The king had a daughter born to him after one of his adulterous affairs. She was illegitimate. Her name was Elizabeth Tudor, and, after many years, she fell in line to be the only candidate to be crowned Queen of England. And on that memorable day Elizabeth Tudor was ushered into Westminster Abbey. It was jam-packed with people. Whispers, innuendoes, suggestive remarks filled that stately Cathedral, "She's illegitimate, and she is not worthy."

Suddenly, two knights, one on either side, rode in on two battle horses, dressed in armor. Then the door swung open and Sir Edwin Dymoke, the mightiest knight in England, sitting on the finest charger, rode through those doors, down the aisle, into the interior of the Church, and stood in front of Elizabeth Tudor. You literally could have heard a pin drop. This power specimen of humanity threw down the gauntlet and said "Elizabeth Tudor is Queen of England, and, if any man contests this, do it now." With his sword drawn he waited, but there was not a sound. Suddenly the horns blew, and he spurred his white charger and rode out. And Queen Elizabeth I reigned for over fifty years!

In the truest sense we were all born illegitimate for from the beginning; Jesus said our father was the devil. For in sin did our mothers conceive us. We carried the guilt. We carried the shame, and all the reproach was ours. But at Calvary, Jesus took the guilt. He took the shame, and the reproach was laid upon Him. "He raiseth up the poor out of the dust, and lifteth up the beggar from the dunghill, to set them among princes, and to make them inherit the throne of glory" (I Samuel 2:8).

The Bible calls Satan "The accuser of the brethren." He will accuse you night and day. He can shoot his flaming arrows of condemnation from now till doomsday. But there is coming a day, soon and very soon, that the heavens will roll back like a scroll. Heaven's Knight in shinning armor will ride in on His snow-white, lighting-fast charger with His laser light sword drawn. He will turn to the devil and the host of hell and say, "If any or all of you contest this, do it now." But remember: You will not deal with them. You will deal directly with me."

There will not be a sound or whisper of any accusation. Then the trumpet will sound, and we will rise out of this world to be crowned as kings in the kingdom of Christ to help Him rule for a thousand years. And forever we will be with the Lord of Glory.

We have accurately gone from the depths of depravity to the pinnacle of paradise, from the lowest hell to the highest heaven. As King David put it so eloquently many, many years ago in Psalms 40:2-3, "He brought me up also out of an horrible pit, out of the miry clay, and set my feet upon a rock, and established my goings. And he hath put a new song in my mouth, even praise unto our God: many shall see it, and fear, and shall trust in the LORD." I guess you could say we have gone from the mire to the choir!

CHAPTER TEN

HAVE YOU HEARD ANY GOOD NEWS LATELY?

IN THE FIRST Church of the Chosen Frozen, better known as the Church of the Living Dead, there arose a problem. The icicle they called the pastor resigned. He had been there for forty freezing years, and he ran what could be called a "smoothie" operation. The ushers were trained to skate up the isle every Sunday picking up cold cash. The music minister had a striking resemblance to the cruise director from the Titanic. The greeters at the door moved with such efficiency that you could almost see dead lice falling from them. Dr. Sounding Brass was beyond reproach, but his sermons were beyond the understanding of the common man. He really wanted to stay and ride the church down to nothing and then retire, but the effects of frostbite forced him into early retirement. So the petrified parishioners formed a search committee to locate and secure a new preacher. After six months of screening and interviews the committee agreed almost unanimously to call a young, wiry, little preacher from Oklahoma.

The long awaited day had arrived and the new pastor opened his Bible and took his text from Romans, Chapter one, Verse Sixteen: "For I am not ashamed of the gospel of Christ: for it is the power of God unto salvation to every one that believeth; to the Jew first, and also to the Greek." Then he announced his title with clear and exciting articulation, "Folks, today I am going to preach on the subject "*The Gospel*!" For the next forty minutes he preached like a dying man to dying people. In the south it is what is called, "Shucking corn." The church was energized and the pulpit committee was proud of their wise choice.

The next Sunday the congregation returned and sat in their pews with bated breath, just to hear another fiery sermon from their new preacher. He again mounted the pulpit, and to their surprise, he announced again, "Today, ladies and gentlemen, I am going to preach on the subject, "*The Gospel*!" Then with the same zeal he preached the identical sermon he had preached the week before. The congregation enjoyed it again, but not as much, and the committee was a little let down. However, they were optimistic and said, "Surely he will preach a different sermon next Sunday."

Next Sunday came and for the third week in a row the young, stimulating pastor preached from the same text, the same title and the same sermon. By this time the committee, to say the least, was ticked off. They had a secret meeting in the afternoon and discussed their problem. They came to the conclusion they would have to talk to the new pastor, so they elected Mr. Big Bucks to go to the parsonage and explain their feelings.

The elected member went to the parsonage and knocked on the door. The pastor opened the door and greeted the board member and invited him in. Once inside, the Elder opened the conversation, "Pastor, we are so proud you have come to our church. Your first sermon on the Gospel was superb, and the whole church was blessed. We were a little surprised that you preached the same sermon the second week, and we endured. However, I speak for the committee and the congregation. Three weeks in a row was too much. Don't you have another sermon? Why don't you preach on a subject that will grow our little church? Something that will communicate to the upper crust of our community and gain their attention. Why don't you preach on a subject that will reach out and grab the attorneys, the judges, the doctors, the college professors and the philosophers? Something contemporary and put that old out dated sermon up."

The young preacher thought about it for a moment and said, "You know, you may be right. I believe I will preach on something that will draw the movers and shakers of our city. Next Sunday I am going to preach on "*Pills*."" So, they put it in the paper, on the marquee, and on the radio, "Come to the First Church of the Chosen Frozen; This Sunday the Preacher is going to preach on "*Pills!*""

Sunday the church was full, and, sure enough, the upper echelon of society was there. From the mayor to the school board, they were all there to hear the sermon on *pills*. The anticipated moment finally came, and the pastor took the podium looked out at his distinguished guests and said, "I want to thank everyone that is here today, and, as I promised, I am going to preach on "*Pills*."" The committee looked at each other with a sly grin of accomplishment. The pastor said, "In this big world we live in there are all kinds of pills. There are blue pills; red pills black pills, white pills, orange pills, yellow pills, purple pills and even polka-dotted pills. But, today there is only one pill I know that really works. So today I am going to preach on the "*Gos-pill!*"

The truth is this little preacher like Paul was never ashamed of the Gospel, which is the good news of the kingdom. And, as Paul, we ought to believe in, build upon and broadcast the Gospel every day in every way we possibly can. Someone may ask, just what really is the Gospel? The Gospel in a nutshell is simply the death, the burial, and the resurrection of Christ. Man was placed in a perfect paradise, but he disobeyed

God and was driven to the wild wilderness. The bad news is man fell by disobedience and lost his original state of perfection. But the good news is the second Adam, Jesus Christ, stood tall in temptation and by His obedience to the Father's will bought and brought us back in fellowship with God. The bad news makes the good news good.

One day Cain and Abel came running as fast as their little legs would carry them to their father Adam. Abel said in an excited tone, "Daddy, Daddy, we were playing over by the river and we discovered a wall that we had never seen before. So we climbed it all the way to the top. And, would you believe, we saw the most beautiful and luscious garden, the likes you can't imagine." Then Cain asked, "Dad, do you think we could ever live in such a wonderful place?" Adam replied, "Boys, once upon a time we did until your mother ate us out of house and home!"

To fully understand life you must first understand death. Death is not cessation of life. It is separation from God. Again, God placed the first Adam in the garden and gave him and Eve everything they would ever possibly need to be happy, healthy, and holy. God made provision for their spirit, soul, and body. Now Adam's insubordination to God's command left him defiled in spirit, and the sure and swift consequence to his sin was death. God said, "But of the tree of the knowledge of good and evil, thou shalt not eat of it: for in the day that thou eatest thereof thou shalt surely die" (Genesis 2:17).

To the average observer and especially to the critic, this seems contradictory, or at the least a lie, that the day Adam ate the fruit he didn't drop dead on the spot but lived to the ripe old age of 930. So what did God mean when he said, "Thou shall surely die?" It's simple: Adam died immediately in his spirit. He was immediately cut off from God and His presence. The result was he lost his spiritual covering. Realizing they were naked and he and his wife hid themselves.

Adam died progressively in his soul. Since God was no longer in Adam's tabernacle, his soul in time progressively grew worse to the point his offspring finally angered God to the point of global annihilation of all but Noah and his family that "found grace in the eyes of the Lord." Adam and his descendants became self-centered instead of God-centered. Then Adam died ultimately in his body: "And all the days that Adam lived were nine hundred and thirty years: and he died" (Genesis 5:5).

Adam was like a Christmas tree that was cut from its roots. It was chosen, brought home, decorated with lights, bulbs, and tensile. It looked very much alive. It smelled alive; it felt alive, and, ask little Jr., it even tasted alive for a while. But by the time the holiday festivities were over and the last turkey leg was eaten, by New Year's Day the once beautiful evergreen wasn't green any more. It was turning dead brown because it was dead. It just took a while for death to show its true colors.

This is where the Gospel comes to our rescue. Salvation is not purely just to get you to the Father's house. It is making you the Father's house so God can live inside of you. "Know ye not that ye are the temple of God, and that the Spirit of God dwelleth in you?" (I Corinthians 3:16). The purpose of the Gospel is to not only get us out of earth to heaven, but to get God out of heaven and back in us on earth again. When an individual believes the Gospel and is saved, God puts in reverse the effects and the corollary of sin. Remember Adam died…

Immediately in his Spirit,
Progressively in his Soul, and
Ultimately in his Body.

However when we are born again and become a child of God we are…

Justified Immediately in our Spirits,
Sanctified Progressively in our Souls, and
Glorified Ultimately in our Bodies.

Let me put it in the past, present, and future tense:

1. Past Tense—Justified in your Spirit—Saved from the Penalty of sin
2. Present Tense—Sanctified in your Soul—Saved from the Power of sin
3. Future Tense—Glorified in your Body—Saved from the Possibility of sin.

Death is such a frightening thing to most people because it seems to be final. The fear of death is universal and more terrifying than a horror flick on a Saturday night. There is a certain phobia when it comes to the unspoken topic of death. But the Gospel has come to take the fear out of death. Because the Gospel makes it transparent, we see death for what it really is, a master of deception. Also, we know that Jesus has taken the sting out of death. Without a sting, death can only impersonate the king of terrors because without a sting there is nothing to fear.

When I was a small boy only in the first grade, I learned something that no other kid in my class knew. My dad was a beekeeper, and he taught me that the male bee or the drone did not have a stinger. So on a regular basis he would bring me a drone, and I developed quite a collection. Being of the more mischievous nature, I would bring a few of my prized pets to school—not for show and tell, but for chase and scare or for shock and awe. I had a lot of fun until the teacher caught me, and I had to go see the Principal.

This is precisely what the devil does to most people. He runs around like a roaring lion chasing the huddled masses with the fright of death. But, again, the Gospel reveals at a closer look that death has no sting.

Once a man slipped on some water and hit his head, putting him into a coma. He stayed in the coma for several weeks until the doctors determined he was dead (but their prognosis was incorrect.) They called the funeral director, and he came and took the alleged dead man to the funeral parlor and stuck him in a casket before they embalmed him because they were extremely busy with their dying business. At three o' clock in the morning the alive-dead man woke out of his coma to find himself in a casket lying in a dimly lit room. He then sat up looked around and upon recognizing he was at a funeral home he said to himself, "Good grief! What in the world is going on here? If I am alive what am I doing in this coffin? And if I am dead then why do I need to go to the restroom?"

The celebrated victory of death is a false one! Christ met death at Calvary and for three days and three nights it seemed as though death was the victor. The demons of hell laughed and shouted with glee while Satan sit on his imperial throne thinking himself the dark horse. The shouts could be heard throughout the galactic universe, "Christ is dead, and death and the devil are the winners!"

But after three days of gala a shadow fell across the regions of the damned. And then came Jesus, walking not on water this time, but upon the billowy eternal waves of fire. He walked right up to Satan and confronted "His Majesty the Devil," and said, " I'll take those keys!" The devil said, "Nobody ever has talked to me that way!" Then Jesus said, "Because there has never been anyone like me!" Satan then asked, "Who are you?" And Christ replied, "I am the Resurrection!"

Jesus grabbed the keys of death and hell then kicked the devil off his royal seat and said, "You are where you belong," and slammed the door. He walked directly across corridor, opened up paradise and said, "Come on children. We're are moving up higher!" He broke death, and death has been defeated. Its sting has been extracted and the grave has been robbed of its victory.

One elderly saint was dying and the good doctor said to her family, "It won't be long Now. She is sinking fast." Suddenly, for a moment, she regained presence of mind and replied, "Young man, I am not sinking, I am rising! I can't sink because I'm on the Rock!"

Again, this is the good news of the Gospel, the death, the burial, and the resurrection of Jesus Christ. The Gospel gives us seven unshakable, unwavering, and unbelievable timely and eternal benefits.

1. The Gospel Denounces Sin

Because of the fall, we were born with a sinful nature and that nature clouds the evilness of sin. But the Gospel has come to reveal the wickedness that sin really is. It openly denounces it in its tracks. The world treats sin as a joke. They see no wrong in any sin. Even sins as perverted and distorted as homosexuality the world christens an alternate lifestyle. But God explicitly calls it an abomination and a sin to be judged as such at the Great White Throne.

Today's world is not much different than the world Noah lived in. As a matter of fact, Jesus said it would revert back to that before His coming. The cup of sin had gotten so full that the Lord regretted that He made man. So God pushed the cup over and poured out His judgment and the whole world was lost, except Noah and his family, all because of the iniquity of sin.

The day has come that men call evil good and good evil. Anyone that calls sin what it is today is automatically labeled hateful of people, inconsiderate, intolerant, predatory, and almost put in the same category as Adolph Hitler. The twisted evil minds of men have even called the Bible a book of detestation and anyone who preaches it a minister of hate. Mankind has fallen to the lowest level of iniquity, and the saddest fact of it all is they don't have a clue that they are there.

This is why Christ commissioned us to take the Gospel to the ends of the earth. "And he said unto them, Go ye into all the world, and preach the gospel to every creature. He that believeth and is baptized shall be saved; but he that believeth not shall be damned" (Mark 16:15–16).

We need a true concept of sin and a vision of sin as seen through the eyes of God. If you sow the seeds of sin, God says you will reap the weeds of sin. With God it is black and white, but our generation has turned it into a pretty gray. Even so, the Gospel denounces sin and shows us what sin really is.

2. The Gospel Displays the Savior

Now, if God only showed us our sin and said, "Tough luck," or "Sorry I wish I could help," we would be without hope in this world. Just as God commanded Noah to build an ark to save himself and his family from the watery torrents of judgment, God has sent His only begotten Son to be the New Testament Ark for those who believe. Noah had to believe the voice of God just as we must believe the Word of God. "For God so loved the world, that he gave his only begotten Son, that whosoever believeth in him should not perish, but have everlasting life. For God sent not his Son into the world to condemn the world; but that the world through him might be saved" (John 3:16–17).

The Gospel wouldn't be the Gospel without a Savior. What would the Gospel be like without the story of Jesus? How He was born of a virgin and lived a sinless life. How He was betrayed with a kiss by one of His own disciples and gave Himself to the Sanhedrin on the darkest night of human infamy. How He was turned over to the Romans to be beaten like a dog and then crucified like deranged murderer. What would the Gospel be like without the thorns, the cross, the spikes, and the blood?

Without a sacrificing Savior there wouldn't be a Gospel. It would only be bad news, and then the bad news would only get worse. But, praise God, the Gospel displays the Savior. He that has eyes, let him see!

3. The Gospel Delivers Salvation

We need a Savior because we need salvation.

> The Body needs Salvation for Direction,
> The Spirit needs Salvation for Determination,

The Soul needs Salvation for Destiny.

The Gospel (the death, the burial and the resurrection of Jesus) delivers God's salvation to man. Salvation is redemption, and redemption is deliverance. Someone may ask, "Deliverance from what?" Deliverance from sin and its awful consequences. We have a...

Shield of Salvation,
Rock of Salvation,
Tower of Salvation,
Horn and buckler of Salvation, and
Helmet of Salvation.
And thank God for the Joy of Salvation!
We have salvation from...

the Curse of the Law,
Condemnation,
Coming Judgment,
A Guilty Conscience,
The Fear of Death,
A Wasted Life, and
the Bondage of Sin.

God has given us complete and full salvation. It has not been given to us on an installment plan—a little now and a little later. God has given us complete and full salvation. He is able to pull us from the gutter most and save us to the uttermost, then He seals us unto the day of redemption. That is why Paul the Apostle said with an iron clad guarantee, "For the which cause I also suffer these things: nevertheless I am not ashamed: for I know whom I have believed, and am persuaded that he is able to keep that which I have committed unto him against that day" (II Timothy 1:12). What day was he speaking of? The day he stood in God's judgment. Not only would he be sound and safe, but also he would be saved.

4. The Gospel Dispenses Success

When an individual turns from God, that individual is stripped of the best he could ever develop into. He may enjoy a good life and have a lot of positive things going on for him, but if he is rejecting Jesus Christ, he is absolutely being robbed of the very best he could ever become. Paul gives testimony to this when he said,

> Circumcised the eighth day, of the stock of Israel, of the tribe of Benjamin, an Hebrew of the Hebrews; as touching the law, a Pharisee; Concerning zeal, persecuting the church; touching the righteousness which is in the law, blameless. But what things were gain to me, those I counted loss for Christ. Yea, doubtless, and I count all things but loss for the excellency of the knowledge of Christ Jesus my Lord: for whom I have suffered the loss of all things, and do count them but dung, that I may win Christ (Philippians 3:5–8).

What Paul is saying is that with all his credentials and pure pedigree, he did not know anything about success until he believed the Gospel.

Jesus demonstrated this in His first miracle at the wedding in Cana of Galilee. He turned the water into wine. But there was more to the miracle than changing one substance into another. It was the detail that this wine was better wine than the wine that had been served. Simply, Jesus made better wine! Everything Jesus makes is the best. Everything about Christ has quality. Christians are not an inferior grade of people; the Christian life has quality to it, and it is enhanced with the aroma of success. He takes you the way you are and makes you better. You may be good water in the pot, but when Jesus gets a hold of you, you'll be better wine in the cup!

I have heard people say, "I would be a Christian, but I don't want to be less." You cannot be less. You will always be more. This Blind eye Opener, this Water Walker and this Wine Maker will always leave you better than when He found you. This old thing, "Well, I would be a Christian, but I just really want to be something," is a lie and a sham. You can't be a better something than the light of the world or the salt of the earth. You can't get any better than the sons of God or heirs with God and joint heirs with Jesus Christ.

The Gospel dispenses success because it gives you a...

foundation to stand upon

Friend to lean upon,

Family to be a part of, and

Future to look forward to.

5.   The Gospel Defeats Satan

Many people I have known have what I call "devil phobia." They are afraid of the devil. A man was on his way to a masquerade party dressed as the devil in a red suit. Suddenly a storm arose, pouring down a torrential rain that caused him to seek the nearest shelter, which happened to be a church. When he opened the door, everyone in the church turned all the way around to see who the latecomer was, only to be shocked by the sight of the devil. Without a script, the women screamed out in unison, and the men and children made a mad dash for the nearest exit. Everyone in the church was gone in a blaze except one woman who got stuck in her pew. She was frozen in her tracks like a deer caught in the headlights of a car. The man in the devil suit slowly walked down the aisle and stopped right beside her. She was too frightened so she just kept her head looking straightforward. Then she said, "Hello, Mr. Devil. I know you know I have been going to this church for fifty years. But I know you also know, I've been on your side the whole time!"

The nation seems to be entranced by the demonic. The obsession has given rise to movies that portray a strong theme of the supernatural and spiritual world. This allurement is a double-edge sword: For many it has provided entertainment, yet also it has created a natural fear for the devil. But God has sent us the Gospel, and the Gospel is the only thing that can and will handle Satan.

Satan is the master intimidator. The Bible gives a metaphor of the devil as a "roaring lion seeking whom he may devour" (I Peter 5:8). The purpose of the roar is to intimidate every living creature in the jungle. That roar seems to make the lion larger than life. So we tend to make Satan more powerful than he really is. Admittedly, Satan has power, but don't ever forget, Jesus has all power. That's why the Scripture admonishes us, "O magnify the LORD with me, and let us exalt his name together" (Psalms 34:3).

That is not to make the Lord bigger than He is. You cannot make God bigger than He is; that is impossible. Articulate all the words you can dream up, and when you have run out of adjectives and your mind has wandered to the twilight zone and back, God is still bigger! The secret in magnifying the Lord is not to make Him bigger than He is but to see Him bigger than you have ever seen Him. Without the Gospel you will naturally upon instinct make Satan bigger than he really is.

When my daughter Shanta was around four or five years old she came running to me screaming, "Daddy, Daddy, there is an octopus!" She was pointing to the floor just in front of my bookcase. So I walked over and knelt down to see what was giving her such a fright. There, crawling; was a small spider about the size of a green pea. I must admit, if you were to magnify that little spider a million times, it would have taken on the spitting image of the octopus from the movie, "Twenty Thousand Leagues Under the Sea." But take the microscope off, and it was just a little non-venomous spider. So I smashed it with the bottom of my shoe.

As long you magnify Satan he will loom as large as the Empire State Building on the horizons of your life. The Gospel brings the devil down to size. Jesus said, "I beheld Satan as lightning fall from heaven. Behold, I give unto you power to tread on serpents and scorpions, and over all the power of the enemy: and nothing shall by any means hurt you" (Luke 10:18–19). With the Gospel at your disposal the only soul the devil will ever touch is the sole of your shoe! Put the devil under your foot with the power of the Gospel!

6.   The Gospel Delights With Satisfaction

There was this lawyer in Dallas, Texas, who was opening the door of his brand new BMW 740i when a car from behind came flying by and hit it, ripping the door off its hinges. The police arrived and found the lawyer jumping up and down with rage, yelling bitterly about the damage to his precious, expensive car. "You lawyers are so materialistic, you make me sick," a police officer commented, shaking his head in repulsion. Then he said, "You're so worried about your beautiful BMW that you didn't even notice that your left arm was ripped off." "Oh, no!" said the lawyer, looking down and noticing the bloody stump where his arm had been. "Where's my Rolex?"

I think of all the people who ever lived, Jesus knew more about the subject of satisfaction than anyone else. With a keen eye of perspective Jesus said, "Take heed, and beware of covetousness: for a man's life consisteth not in the abundance of the things which he possesseth" (Luke 12:15). How did He know? It is simple; He was the Creator from the dawn of human conception.

Possessions have never satisfied the deep longing of the soul. The Architect didn't design you that way. God made man a living soul that is housed in a body. He did not make you a living body. You are not your body; the real you lives on the inside. Therefore, tangible material things will not bring satisfaction. We all know and are fully aware that things are like a drug—they will bring a momentary thrill. But like a drug, things will lift you way up then slam you way down. One man said, "I love the smell of those new cars. But I hate those stinking payments." It is true the new wears off, many times before we have made the first payment.

I recently heard of a woman who bought a parrot to keep her company. She took him home, but returned the bird to the store the next day.

"This bird doesn't talk," she told the owner.

"Does he have a mirror in his cage?" asked the owner, "Parrots love mirrors. They see themselves in the mirror and start up a conversation."

The woman bought a mirror and left. The next day, she returned. The bird still wasn't talking.

"How about a ladder? Parrots love walking up and down a ladder. A happy parrot is more likely to talk."

The woman bought a ladder and left.

Sure enough, she was back the next day; the bird still wasn't talking.

"Does your parrot have a swing? If not, that's the problem. He'll relax and talk up a storm."

The woman reluctantly bought a swing and left.

When she walked into the store the next day, her countenance had changed.

"The parrot died," she said.

The pet store owner was shocked.

"I'm so sorry. Tell me, did the parrot ever say a word?" he asked.

"Yes, right before he died," the woman replied. "He said, 'Don't they sell any food down at that pet store?'"

Things, possessions, money, and materialism were never in the master design to fill or fulfill satisfaction to the man inside the body. The Gospel is the only thing on this revolving green and blue planet that can fill the hunger of the human soul of man. Now if things won't make us happy, why do we believe more things will make us more happy? If you will feed your spiritual man the Gospel, you will have unlocked the secret men have been looking for ever since Adam was kicked out of the garden. The Gospel is the only thing that has ever or will ever delight the soul with satisfaction.

7. The Gospel Determines Our Security

If you haven't already noticed, life is filled with swift transition. On life's journey the winds can change direction so quickly your head will swim. The waves can grow larger, and your whole world can change in an instant. The potential is ever before us of going from…

Calm to Chaos,
Docility to Disarray,
Control to Confusion, or
Placid to Pandemonium.

We were in the 6th grade between classes at Central Middle School in Oklahoma City. Gary Dawson, Robert Mithcum, and I were walking down a long hall in single file, in that order. This was the mid-70's when busing in Oklahoma had just begun. The racial tension was thick between the white kids and the black kids. So as we walked down that long hallway, a sea of African American students met us. When out of nowhere came a voice rang out above the shuffling of feet, "Get you one, Theodus!" Then a big black fist came crushing into the left side of Robert Mitchum's face. Retaliation was impossible, taken the differences of size and number, so we just walked on. All I have to say is, "Poor Robert." You have days like that, when you're minding your own business and concentrating on what is before you when out of nowhere, you get punched in the face. We used to call that, "Getting thumped!"

Interestingly enough, I learned years later that, after a potter makes a pot, he bakes the pot. After he fires the pot in the furnace, then he must check it. He pulls it out of the fire and gives it a thump, from which they have coined a phrase, "Getting thumped." Now the reaction of the pot determines its destiny. If it sings (that is the potter's term), it is ready to become a purposeful vessel. But, if it thuds (again the this is the potter's term), it is not ready; it must immediately go back into the oven.

When you get thumped, how do you react? Do you sing, or do you thud? Do you get bitter, or do you get better? Do you pout with pessimistic sarcasm, or do you sing with optimistic security? The Gospel will give you the security to know, "And we know that all things work together for good to them that love God, to them who are the called according to [his] purpose" (Romans 8:28).

Knowing God has a plan and design for your life gives you a built in security that you can't get any other place. All thumps work for your good in the Gospel plan. And God wants to use you "If a man therefore purge himself from these, he shall be a vessel unto honour, sanctified, and meet for the master's use, [and] prepared unto every good work" (II Timothy 2:21).

My wife and I had dinner with Robert Mitchum and his wife twenty-five years after that dreadful day in Central Middle School. During our delightful evening that subject surfaced during our candlelight dinner. I reminded him of "Get you one, Theodus!" and we had a great laugh.

Paul tells us in II Corinthians 5:8–9, "We are confident, [I say], and willing rather to be absent from the body, and to be present with the Lord. Wherefore we labour, that, whether present or absent, we may be accepted of him." Where do we find this confidence, (which is just another word for security)? In the Gospel! We have nothing to dread and nothing to fear we have the Gospel.

The story is that an old Scottish man was dying when he was met at his bedside by his little grandson. His grandson asked his dying grandpa, "Grandpa, are you afraid to die?" To that the old man said, "No, son, for you see, while I was on this earth living, Jesus was with me. Now, I am dying and He is still with me, and, when I die, I am leaving this earth, and I am going to be with Jesus." How simple, but, oh, how true. Now that is good news any way you slice it!

CHAPTER ELEVEN

ON A CLEAR DAY YOU CAN SEE FOREVER

THERE IS AN ancient legend of a rich merchant from Samaria who went to Baghdad to buy supplies. Once he was there he sent his servant into the market place to purchase the allotted items from a list. The servant while in the hustling market place accidentally jostled an old lady, and, when she turned around, he recognized her as Death. She then gave the rich man's servant a very threatening gesture. The servant ran back immediately to his master and begged for allowance to return to Samaria. He said, "Master, while I was in the market place, I by accident jostled an old lady, and, when she turned around, I knew instantly she was Death. She gave me a very threatening gesture. Please have mercy and give me your fastest steed and allow me to flee my fate at once!" The master said, "Go!" The servant then mounted the fastest, most fleet-footed horse in the caravan and rode like the wind back to his beloved Samaria. The rich man then went himself into the market place, found the old lady, reached and grabbed her by the arm turning her quickly around. He also recognized her as Death. Then he asked Death this question, "Why did you give my servant such a threatening gesture?" To that Death replied, "That was not a threatening gesture at all. It was a look of surprise for I was surprised to see your servant in Baghdad. I have an appointment with him tonight in Samaria!"

The Bible enunciates this truth, "And as it is appointed unto men once to die, but after this the judgment," (Hebrews 9:27 27). You may be late for your medical appointment, your dinner appointment, or for your wedding appointment, but you will be right on time for your appointment with death. Death is unavoidable, and you will not be late for it. Tomorrow will never die, but you will.

Why is it so easy to believe that others will die but it is so difficult to believe we will die? As someone has said, "All men think all men are mortal but themselves." Death is the only thing certain about life. The preacher was preaching on heaven as his Sunday morning subject when in the middle of his sermon he stopped and asked this pivotal question: "Who in this church wants to go to heaven?" Everyone raised a hand except one little nine-year-old boy. So the preacher looked down at him and asked, "Son, you mean you don't want to go to heaven?" "Why yes," replied the little boy. "Then pray tell me why you did not raise your hand?" With all sincerity the boy answered, "Well, preacher, the way you put it I thought you were getting up a boat load today!" Everyone wants to go to heaven, but no one wants to die.

Life is filled with good news/bad news scenarios. The good news is everyone who is saved and washed in the blood of Jesus Christ is going to heaven. The bad news is you have to die to get there. The fact must be settled: Outside of the rapture of the church the local cemetery stands as an every day reminder that at any moment you could die, and you will die eventually. You may not die today, but you will die another day. When you finally come to grips with the reality that death is unavoidable and your faith is unmovable, you can stand flatfooted, throw your shoulder back, cock your head up, and with a twinkle in your eye stare death in the face and shout in the mouth of hell, "O death where is your victory, O grave where is your sting!" The resurrection of Christ assures the immortality of the soul. You really cannot live until first you overcome the fear of death.

The Greatest of all Fears is: The fear of death.
  The Greatest of all Fantasies is: The hope of immortality.
    The Greatest of all Facts is: Jesus conquered death and gives immortality to the soul.

Jesus pronounced death on death, conquered the fear of death, extracted the sting of death, opened up a superhighway and said,

> Follow me, and I will take you to the Father." "Let not your heart be troubled: ye believe in God, believe also in me. In my Father's house are many mansions: if it were not so, I would have told you. I go to prepare a place for you. And if I go and prepare a place for you, I will come again, and receive you unto myself; that where I am, there ye may be also (John 14:1–3).

An evangelist had come to the church to win souls and get people ready for heaven. During his red-hot, fiery sermon he made this striking point: "Every member of this church will die!"

As soon as he said this, he noticed a man about half way back peel off a sheepish grin, which disturbed the evangelist. So he repeated the phrase.

This time the man nearly broke out in open laughter that disturbed the preacher even more. One more time the evangelist repeated the phrase with all the authority and gusto he possessed. This time the man let out an uncontrolled belly laugh that was heard all through the church.

After the service the evangelist caught the man at the water fountain and really let him have it.

"What in God's world do you think is so funny in the fact that every member of this church will die?"

"I am not a member of this church," the man replied.

It is clear to see this man completely missed the point, wouldn't you say? But don't you miss the point; you will die. The last time I checked the mortality rate is still at 100%. Everyone who drinks water will die.

But dying is not the end of the world if you live in hope the resurrection. It is not as bad as you think. Of course, I am saying this not from a personal experience but from the viewpoint of faith. Jesus Christ who conquered the last fortress on the frontier of life made us this promise: "I am the resurrection, and the life: he that believeth in me, though he were dead, yet shall he live: And whosoever liveth and believeth in me shall never die" (John 11:25–26). Jesus went into the grave and beyond, but He came back to say, "That whosoever believeth in him should not perish, but have eternal life" (John 3:15).

I believe that when death happens and it's over, we will say, "That was it? If I had only known." A few years ago I developed a cavity in one tooth. I kept putting going to the dentist off because I have a phobia for shots—especially in my mouth. But the time came when I could put off going no longer. The pain was unendurable. On my appointment day I sat in the chair closed my eyes, opened my mouth, and in my mind I begged God for mercy for fear of the needle. Dr. Whitehead began to work, and I could feel him getting ready. But I didn't dare open my eyes. In about two to three minutes he took his hands and instruments out of my mouth. I then opened my eyes and said, "Doc, what happened. Don't do me this way. Let's get it over with and just do it." He then said, "Preacher, it's all over." "You mean you already gave me the shot?" "That's it?" His hygienist said, "The Doctor learned to take the sting out of the shot while studying in college!" And then she added, "And he is good!" To that I replied "Amen!"

What you have put off all your life, that is your appointment with death, when your appointment day arrives and you close your eyes and you open them again, you will have felt nothing but grace. Jesus will say, "It is over. You have made it. Welcome to my Fathers house." You may say, "Whoa, wait just a minute. You mean that which I have been afraid of all my life is over? That was it? That was the King of Terrors?" Jesus will probably say, "That is what I have tried to tell you all of your life. Because I live, ye shall live also" (John 14:19). Jesus Christ is the Great Physician, and He took the sting out of death. And may I add, "He is good!"

Heaven is neither a myth, a mirage, or a madman's dream. Heaven is a place. "I go to prepare you a place, that where I am there you may be also" (John 14:2–30). During my first pastorate, I would go by the retirement center just down the street from our church and give the residents there a short devotion, just to be a blessing and to give them the encouragement to keep the faith. There was one little lady whose name I have long forgotten, but I called her "Questions." Before I would leave, she would always ask me questions. Her usual scheme was to ask me a question in order to stump me and make it appear that she got one over on the preacher. It was all just fun and games. One morning she asked me in front of everyone, "Preacher, will heaven be on this earth or will heaven be up in the sky?" I knew what she had found, a question that could be interpreted either way, so no matter how I answered it she could point out the error of my answer. So I answered, "Questions, I really do not know if heaven will be on the earth or in the sky I haven't been there yet. But I do know this, wherever Jesus is, is where I will be, and, if Jesus is there, that will be heaven to me."

With all honesty it makes me little difference if there are no jasper walls or pearly gates or if the streets of the city are dirt roads and the mansions are three by three canvas tents. If Jesus is there, that will be heaven to me!

But those mansions Jesus spoke of are not three by three canvas tents nor are they six by six cardboard shanties; they are mansions on the God scale. I have seen earth's mansions with all the glitter, gold, and grandeur. But do you really think the finite pea- brains of men can out-think, out-engineer, and out-build God?

God stepped out on *no place* and reached into *nowhere* and grabbed *nothing* and flung it across *nowhere* and said, "Stay there," and it did! And just look at the magnificence of God in the crown of creation.

But again that is on earth. Can you imagine what heaven is like? No. We really can't because our capacity to know is way too small. If you compare a thimble of water to the vastness of uncharted oceans, then you begin to get just a glimpse of the incomparableness of God. The White House, Buckingham Palace, and the Taj Mahal do not even qualify for my doghouse in heaven.

Notice Jesus said, "Many mansions" (John 14:2). There is room for everyone. Heaven is not some crowded ghetto or some backstreet slum where six families live in a two hundred square foot apartment. It is not some roachville where they leave the light on just to keep the critters at bay. It is classified as a mansion, the likes you can't even imagine. "But as it is written, Eye hath not seen, nor ear heard, neither have entered into the heart of man, the things which God hath prepared for them that love him" (I Corinthians 2:9). Just think if the street and driveway that lead up to the mansion are solid gold, what will the mansion be like? I have only one thing to say, "Sweet Shangri- La!" A mansion comes as a standard bonus with everyone's salvation. The minute you get saved, a mansion is prepared for you. Now why would anyone trade his or her mansion for crack-cocaine, a bottle of pills, a gambling addiction or another man's wife? The world will fade like an ice cream cone in a furnace, but following God's will leads you to a mansion which is eternal and will never pass away.

Over the years there has arisen a great debate over the word "mansion" as spoken of by Jesus. Many Greek scholars have implanted in our minds that in the original Bible language it really doesn't say, "Mansions," it says "Rooms." This takes away from the concept of individual housing arrangements. Not long ago I watched a documentary on "The World's

Most Expensive Hotel Rooms." They had for the pleasure of the viewing audience a multi-level, three-story hotel room. It was seven thousand square feet and the cost was fifteen thousand dollars a night. I concluded that in order for my wife and me to stay there they would have to leave more than the little chocolate mints; they would have to leave Bill Gates' Visa Gold card with unlimited spending on our pillows.

So, if it is a mansion or if it is a room, who really cares? For, you see, we will be getting a new tabernacle, new housing arrangements for the soul. Here on this earth hair turns white, teeth loose grip, limbs become weak, eyes become dim, and minds become slow, dull, and cloudy. But that is here, not in heaven. In my Father's house, there will be no canes, cataracts, or cardiac arrests. No glass eyes or eye-glasses. No hearing aids, hair pieces, braces or bridges. No pacemakers, peace takers, or party poopers. No defaulters, deliberators, defibrillators, dying, or disease. The blind will see; the deaf will hear; the lame will walk; the mute will speak; the cough will be silenced; the wrinkle will be smoothed, and nothing shall make us afraid!

We will pass behind the curtain and live on and on and on. We will get a brand new body, not one like this. Not one with a wrinkled brow and dimming eyes. Not one with a twisted spine or a withered arm. Not one with an amputated leg or an injured back. Not one with a mind haunted over past failures. Not one with a heart eaten out with bitter memories or filled with the broken glass of vanquished dreams. No, no, no, not with one of these maladies will we make our grand entrance into the story land. We will rise not clothed again with dying clay, not garbed once more in the fading garments of mortal flesh. But we will rise with the shining mercy of God.

> Behold, I shew you a mystery; We shall not all sleep, but
> we shall all be changed, In a moment, in the twinkling
> of an eye, at the last trump: for the trumpet shall sound,
> and the dead shall be raised incorruptible, and we shall be

changed. For this corruptible must put on incorruption, and this mortal must put on immortality. So when this corruptible shall have put on incorruption, and this mortal shall have put on immortality, then shall be brought to pass the saying that is written, Death is swallowed up in victory O death, where is thy sting? O grave, where is thy victory? (I Corinthians 15:51–55).

We will share in His resurrection, and we will be free forever; free from drag, debt, and dying; free from seduction, temptation and the tempter; free without the possibility of pain, persecution, or problem. We will stand on the pinnacle of paradise and shout with a voice so strong that it will shake the celestial spheres, "Free at last, free at last, thank God Almighty, I'm free at last!"

The Bible gives us a small glimpse of those new bodies. It says in no uncertain terms that we who are faithful will receive a body just like the body Jesus received after His resurrection. He was met by Mary after He arose from the dead. "Jesus saith unto her, Touch me not; for I am not yet ascended to my Father: but go to my brethren, and say unto them, I ascend unto my Father, and your Father; and [to] my God, and your God" (John 20:17).

Piecing the true story together, we read that before the women could return to Jerusalem, Jesus walked through the wall where His disciples were huddled together in fear, sat down, and ate a piece of fish. When they recognized it was the Lord, they fell to the floor, held Him by the feet, and worshiped Him. He spoke with them, got up, and walked back through the wall. I know how Jesus got through the wall, but I have never been able to figure out how that fish got back through the wall.

When we look at the stars in the vastness of this universe, we measure them by light years. Light travels at 186 thousand miles per second. That is 668 million miles per hour. The nearest star outside of the sun is Alpha Centauri, and it would take four light years to reach it. If we took off and traveled at the speed of light (668 miles per hour), it would take four years—that is if we didn't stop to rest, go to the restroom, or get a bite to eat. This is only the journey to the nearest star.

As matter of fact, when you look up on a clear night, you can see stars with the naked eye that are one hundred light years away. If you jet rocketed off at 668 million miles an hour and traveled for a century, you would reach some. But you would still not reach heaven.

Astronomers tell us there are stars that are millions of light years away, and heaven is beyond them. Jesus left the tomb and told Mary, "Don't touch me. I haven't ascended to my Father." He left right after daylight for heaven and was back before breakfast. Now that's the kind of body I'm talking about!

Can you imagine a city without a hospital, doctor's office, funeral home, or cemetery? To live in a world without a jail, police officer, or penitentiary seems to be a fairytale. But, believe you me, heaven is a place, and it is real. It has no taxes, gas, electric or water bills; no schools of learning or rehab centers. But the best thought is. That heaven will be a place of eternal tranquility without the fear of terrorism or the threat of war. We will beat our swords into ploughshares and our guns into golf clubs. As they used to sing, "We'll study war no more."

History is one of life's little pleasures for me. I am a true lover of history. I was born in Virginia, and Virginia is rich with history. There is a little place there in Virginia called Appomattox courthouse. It was where the Civil War ended. I was reading not long ago about a young soldier. Private Joshua O. Johns was General Robert E. Lee's personal messenger and courier. He carried all kinds of messages. When Lee sent word to Grant that he desired terms for surrender, he sent Private Johns and his aide. He told them, "I want you to go into Appomattox and find a house suitable for General Grant and I to meet." They arrived in Appomattox and they met a man in the street. The man, Wilbur McClain, showed them an old house, and they told him, "That won't do." Seeing a big brick house across the street, they asked, "Whose is that one?" He said,

"That is my house." They said they wanted to see it. Having seen it, they decided it would serve the purpose very well.

Here is a side note and a very interesting morsel of history: The first battle of the Civil War was fought at Bull Run at Manassas, Virginia. On the battleground is a house not far from where Thomas Jackson received his nickname that has forever been associated with his name, "Stonewall." The house belonged to Wilbur McClain. After the first battle Mr. McClain moved his family to Appomattox for fear that the War Between the States would continue to be fought outside his home. So the Civil War literally began in Wilbur McClain's yard and ended in his living room. General Lee, General Longstreet, and others made their way to Appomattox. Johns rode with them. When the officers got down off their horses, Private O. Johns held the reins of the officer's horses and watched the officers disappear into the house. He said that as he stood there, all those years of war started running through his mind. He thought about all those messages he had carried and all those errands that he had run. Suddenly the thought occurred to him, "Next time I see the General, my war will be over."

The great Apostle Paul had that same testimony. He had been a good soldier for Jesus Christ the Great General's personal messenger and he had faithfully carried that message all over the known world. He had come through hail and high water, been shipwrecked, stoned, snake-bitten, beaten, whipped, and left for dead on many occasions. Now he stares out of a prison cell and sees a chopping block. But then he gets a glimpse of his Father's house and declares, "For I am now ready to be offered, and the time of my departure is at hand. I have fought a good fight, I have finished my course, I have kept the faith: Henceforth there is laid up for me a crown of righteousness, which the Lord, the righteous judge, shall give me at that day: and not to me only, but unto all them also that love his appearing (2 Timothy 4:6–8).

What he was saying is, "Next time I see the General, my war will be over."

Listen to me, Christian: If you are in a battle, don't give up, just fight on. For in just a little while the war will be ended and the next time you see the Great General, your war will be over. The Father's house is a house of grace, the place where hearts swell with rapture without remorse, where the soul will heave and sing with satisfaction without a sigh, where our wondering eyes shall be charmed with visions and never weep, the place in which our hands shall be enriched with palms of victory but shall never tremble and our heads shall be encircled with an exceeding weight of glory but shall never ache. In the Father's house rainbows never fade, suns never set, babies never cry and mother's never die.

Her name was Martha, but they all called her Aunt Martie. One day Aunt Martie called Pastor Jim over and said, "I'd like for you to help me plan for my funeral."

Pastor Jim, a bit disturbed because he had such a love for this blessed saint, said, "Aunt Martie, I really don't want to do that; it makes me real uncomfortable."

"But Pastor Jim, you know that I have only been given six months to live. I am well up in years, and I am ready to go to heaven. I don't want to make it hard on my family by waiting to the last minute to make my funeral arrangements. I want you to help me make them today.

Here is what I want to request; I want the song "Amazing Grace" to be sung. I want the Gospel Trio to sing, and I want you to preach. I want to be buried in that favorite blue dress of mine. And, when they put me in the casket, I want you to make sure that in my left hand is my Bible and in my right hand I want a fork."

"Now "Amazing Grace" is a wonderful song, and I completely understand why you would want it sung at your funeral. The Gospel Trio is great group with a powerful anointing, and I understand they always do an outstanding job. I am your pastor, and it would be my privilege to be the preacher. I will do my very best. Oh, and that blue dress by the way is my favorite too; you always look so good in it. Now, Aunt Martie, I understand why you would want your Bible in your left hand, but I cannot for the life of me figure out why you would want a fork in your right hand" he replied.

"Pastor Jim, you remember after church going to the all day dinner on the ground and, when you were through eating and they would come around and pick up your dishes, they would always tell you 'Keep your fork.' The reason they would tell to keep your fork is because something good was about to follow. Dessert was coming. It may be peach cobbler, or it may be homemade ice cream; but, whatever it was, you knew the best was yet to come!

When people come filing past my casket and they ask you about my Bible, you tell them it was my standard for living, my light in the darkness, it was my hope of heaven, my bread of life. And, when they ask you about the fork, you just tell them THE BEST IS YET TO COME!"

We are going to a place where every home is a mansion, the caretakers of the city are angels, and the city director is the book of life.

> Every person you meet will be a Christian.
> Every step will be a thrill.
> Every day will be rapture.
> Every hour will be jubilee.
> Every moment will be a triumph.
> Every meal will be a banquet.
> Every breath will be exhilarating.
> Every smell will be sweet
> Every day will be eternity.

There will be no wickedness to reign. There will be no grief nor graves; no bondage or burials, no troubles or tombs. In my Father's house there will be no orphanages, crises centers, or homes for battered women. Never an unkind word will be spoken, never a divorce, never a molested child, never an aborted baby. In this house of grace there will never be a storm cloud gathered, no farewells, or sad goodbyes.

It is no wonder Aunt Martie said, "The best is yet to come; keep your fork!" Keep the faith, face the enemy, and stay faithful. Cold or heat, rain or shine, just don't lose sight of the Father's house because Jesus left us with the promise, "It will be worth it all when we see Him." So keep your fork, the best is yet to come!

CHAPTER TWELVE

HE DID WALK ON WATER

MAKE NO MISTAKE Jesus is a man of history. There are undeniable facts based upon historical evidence outside of the Bible that in the time of the Roman Empire that there was a Jewish man who lived in Palestine named Jesus. The historical aspect of the Bible can be authenticated by Jewish and Roman history. Even with all the creational confirmation a fool may deny the existence of God, but there is no way the fact that Jesus of Nazareth lived in the chronological time frame that the Bible gives account could be disputed.

However, Jesus is more and so much more than a man of history. He is not just some ancient artifact of the past or some prized piece of antiquity. Jesus is the true and living Son of God who is, and was and is to come. This same Jesus who graced the shores of Galilee, walked on the water, fed the thousands, raised the dead, and rose from the dead Himself is the same Jesus who lives today. God knew you couldn't implement eternal salvation or forgive your own sin—let alone walk on water. So

He sent His only begotten Son, Jesus Christ, who was born of a virgin, lived, died, and was resurrected on the third day. God came near to us! You couldn't be God; so, God became man and that man is Jesus.

The Apostle John was in exile on the isle called Patmos for his testimony of the Lord Jesus Christ when unexpectedly without warning Jesus appeared unto him and said, "I am Alpha and Omega, the beginning and the ending… which is, and which was, and which is to come, the Almighty" (Revelation 1:8). The *Alpha* and *Omega* are the first and the last letters of the Greek alphabet. This would be like saying in English "I am the A and Z." So whatever you are in need of, if you can spell it, He is all that. If you need hope, He is hope. If you need help, He is help. If you need healing, He is healing! He is *Alpha* and *Omega*, the first and the last, the beginning and the end. He is the…

A. Anointing that destroys the yoke
B. Brightness of God's glory
C. Captain of our salvation
D. Deliverer of all mankind
E. Electricity of life that will put ump in your pump
F. Fountain of youth long searched for
G. Great physician that heals the sick without medicine
H. Hell's dread and Heaven's glory
I. I Am that spoke to Moses at the burning bush
J. Judge of all men both great and small
K. Key that unlocks the unsearchable riches of God
L. Light of the world that illuminates the darkness
M. Manna which came from heaven
N. Name above every name
O. Oasis in the desert times of life
P. Peace of God that passes all understanding
Q. Quickening power that raises the dead
R. Revival God's way

S.   Savior, Sanctifier, and Son of God

T.   Ten commandments

U.   Unsearchable riches of God

V.   Victory that overcomes the world

W.   Water that you drink of that you will never thirst again

X.   X-ray therapy for your cancerous soul

Y.   Yoke that is easy

Z.   Zeal of Christianity

Who He is causes men and women to march without price tags leaving mother, father, houses, and lands and disappear for decades to preach the Gospel in earth's far corners. Why? Because He is *Alpha* and *Omega*. He was there when you took your first breath, and He will be standing there when you take your last breath.

At the wedding in Cana of Galilee, Jesus proved and demonstrated He is never without resource. No matter what takes place, He is always adequate for the task. Jesus never fell victim to any circumstance—not one time, not even at the cross. He gave His life, and no man took it. They had run out of wine at the wedding, which was a problem beyond their ability or supply, but not for Christ.

Outside the town of Gadera, the modern Kersa, close by the eastern shore of the Sea of Galilee, Jesus confirmed He is always the master. Jesus and His disciples met a man who was possessed with enough devils to drown two thousand hogs. He came running to meet Jesus with chains hanging all over him, naked, flesh lacerated, screaming at the Son of God. He circled Him like a shark would circle his prey.

But Jesus wasn't intimidated. He never batted an eye. He was never excited or afraid. His pulse never raced because He never doubted His ability to control the situation.

The wisest of the wise came with their questions, but they walked away put down and humiliated. The meanest of the mean came to daunt Jesus, but they walked away meek as a lamb. There has never been a man like Jesus. He is without equal for He is the incomparable Christ! He is incomparable in His...

Person—He stands alone.

Pronouncements—Never man spoke like this man.

Performance—The demonstration of His power stands unrivaled and unchallenged.

Position—He stands in no danger whatsoever of losing His crown as King of Kings.

Jesus is unparalleled; therefore anything you compare Him to always falls short. He is bigger than your imagination, wiser than the wisdom of the wise men, brighter than all the stars of the universe. There may be another Beethoven, Shakespeare, Lincoln, Einstein or Edison, but there will never be another Christ! God only has one Son, and His name is Jesus. He stands alone! The Bible does give the shadowing of Jesus in types and pictures.

JESUS IS THE ROCK: THE FOUNDATION OF LIBERTY

Jesus Christ is the only foundation for salvation. There is no salvation outside of Jesus. If Christ is not the beginning and ending of your salvation, then you have built on the wrong foundation, and you are lost in your sins. "Neither is there salvation in any other: for there is none other name under heaven given among men, whereby we must be saved" (Acts 4:12). There is no system, no creed, no doctrine, or baptism that saves men and women from their sins. Only Jesus can. No man can save you—no priest, pope, or preacher, not even Mary, Jesus's earthly mother because Jesus is the only pass to paradise.

Joining churches, quoting prayers, being good, being involved in moral and humane activity, being religious, being baptized in Jesus's name only, or even being martyred will not cleanse you from your sin. "And ye shall know the truth, and the truth shall make you free" (John 8:32). To know the truth is to know the true and living God through His Son Jesus Christ.

When I was only sixteen years old, I walked into a little house in Oklahoma City, a sinner in bad need of a Savior. Bound and driven by demons, on my way to hell I came in contact with Christ through repentance, and I was changed. I met Christ, and before the sun could come up the next morning I was a brand new creature. Mama had a new son; the world had a new creation, and God had a new preacher.

During the days of the Great Depression several decades ago America was in trouble. Many individuals were espousing various theories to solve the financial, philosophical, and spiritual problems that beset this nation. At a large rally one noted speaker was espousing the so-called glories of socialism. "America," he said, "could find its way out of its dilemma by embracing socialism, and by doing so it would put a brand new coat on every man in America." Then he closed his telling statement with a question. "Can anyone do better than that?" A man stood to his feet and said, "Yes, sir, I know someone who can do better than that. You say Socialism can put a brand new coat on every man in America. Mister, Jesus Christ can put a brand new man in every coat in America!"

In the last fading light of the old Law of Moses, Jesus came at the lowest tide of human history. People were not looking for Jesus. They were only seeking a way to escape the heavy hand of Caesar. It was a time of great depression and great anguish, a time when miracles were dead and religion had lost its anointing. It seemed as though the heavens were all shut up and the door to God was closed. Then came Jesus, not just to open the door but also to be the door and show men to the Father. Buddha said, "I think I can find the way." Mohammad said, "I think of the way." But Jesus stands unflinching and declares unequivocally with a divine certainty, "I am the way!"

JESUS IS THE ROOT—THE FOUNTAIN OF LIFE

The prophet Isaiah said, "For he shall grow up before him as a tender plant, and as a root out of a dry ground" (Isaiah 53:2). If you sow a plant in dry ground, you have signed its death sentence. It will not live; it will surely die. A plant has to have water to live; otherwise, it is impossible to take the nutrients from the soil. But Jesus is the root out of dry ground. Not only was He planted on this planet, but also He lived and prospered. He walked this earth, and the earth could give Him nothing. He took nothing from the soil. Everything He was, is, and did came from Himself. He is life sprung up in a dry and thirsty world.

When you tap into the Root, you will no longer depend on this world for the nourishment of life. The world will not be your sustenance anymore. You feed from the Root, and through the Root comes everything pertinent to live and be alive. You will draw your water from another well.

Jesus stood at a well and spoke to a woman one hot blistery day and pointed to a well of water and said, "Whosoever drinketh of this water shall thirst again" (John 4:13). Then He said speaking of Himself, "But whosoever drinketh of the water that I shall give him shall never thirst; but the water that I shall give him shall be in him a well of water springing up into everlasting life" (John 4:14).

You don't have to be entertained by this world, watch its filthy movies, sing its silly songs, drink its rotten liquor, take its mind-twisting drugs, or worship its man-made idols. You have Christ, and He is all you need. A little girl was attempting to quote the 23rd Psalm said, "The Lord is my Shepherd, and He's all I want!"

JESUS IS THE RESURRECTION—THE FUTURE OF LIVING

To so many people the future looks dim and gloomy, and to say the least, without hope. If your judgment is derived by the outward circumstance of things, I can understand your depression. There is no hope of a future in this world. There are a lot of things that call themselves hope, but if I believed for one moment my hope was in these, I would be discouraged too. My hope is in the Resurrection, Jesus Christ! When Jesus arrived at the tomb of Lazarus as recorded in the eleventh chapter of John's Gospel, Martha met him there and said; "Jesus, if you had been here yesterday, my brother would not have died." She was saying in essence, "Jesus, I believed you were the Resurrection yesterday." Jesus said to her, "Thy brother shall rise again" She responded, "I know that he shall rise again in the resurrection at the last day." Now she was saying, "I know you are the Resurrection tomorrow." I believe Jesus sort of shook his head and slightly bit His bottom lip and with a forced exhale through His nose said, "Martha, can't you see what I am trying to tell you; I am the Resurrection—not just yesterday or tomorrow, but I am the Resurrection today and right now!" And with a voice that proved mastery over death, shook the galaxies, and vibrated the distant regions of outer space He said, "Lazarus, come forth!" Immediately out of the tomb came hopping a full size man mummy.

Our future is as secure as He is, and that's as secure as you can get. You can be as sure of the resurrection as you are that the sun is coming up in the morning. As a matter of fact, you can be even surer than that. The sun and all the celestial stars that saw the first light of creation will one day dwindle like dying candles and be smothered in darkness. But, when time blossoms into infinity, eternity will forever testify of the sureness of God and the Resurrection. You can be just as sure of the future today as you will be able to a thousand years from today.

There were once two boys who snuck into a cemetery with a paper bag to gather walnuts. They stuffed the bag full, climbed up, and sat on the big wall that separated the cemetery and the street. It was tall enough that from the concrete walk that went around the little city of the dead one could not see the top of it.

Another small boy came walking by and happen to hear the other two boys counting out the walnuts. This is what he heard: "This one's mine, and this one's yours', this one's mine, and this one's yours', this one's mine, and this one's yours…"

The boy on the walk couldn't see the other two boys so he came to the conclusion that it was God and the devil in conversation and they were dividing up the souls. He ran to his grandpa's house down the street. In a panic he hit the screen door and didn't stop until he found his grandpa sitting in the living room.

"Grandpa, Grandpa, hurry! Come down to the grave yard. It's God and the devil and they are passing out souls. Hurry, Grandpa, hurry!"

Grandpa didn't believe this could be true, so he explained it to his grandson. "Now, son, you know I am a deacon at the Church, and you know, if this was the day that God and the devil were dividing the souls up, I would know. Nothing goes on in church that I don't know."

But the grandson persisted and nagged until he finally talked his grandpa into going.

In the meantime, in the process of dividing up the walnuts, the boys dropped two walnuts that fell on the walkway beside the wall. Just as the boy and his grandpa were approaching the cemetery, they heard, "This one's mine, and this one's yours; this one's mine, and this one's yours…"

Grandpa raised an eyebrow, and his pacemaker picked up a couple of rapid beats, but he kept walking until they were standing right under the two unseen boys.

Then they heard one of the boys on top of the wall say, "Well, I guess that is all of them."

The other boy replied, "No, there are still two down on the walkway we haven't got. Let's go get them."

Needless to say, Grandpa got some zip in his suspenders and broke several speed records in the 100-yard dash. He saturated that place with his absence and moved muscles he didn't even know he still had! Why? He wasn't as sure of the resurrection as he thought or said he was.

You can be sure of Jesus and secure in the resurrection. Had not Jesus been resurrected there would be no finish to the race or victory to the battle. The future would look pretty bleak and Christianity would have to join the ranks of Hinduism, Islamism, and Buddhism. But we need to shout it until the rafters' shake, angels dance, and demons scream, "Why seek ye the living among the dead? He is not here He is risen!" Christ is risen indeed!

They tell me, if you were to visit Moscow, you could see the body of Nikolai Lenin, leader of the Communist revolution of 1917, Premier of the U.S.S.R. (1917–24). Some people there still worship him. People still go by his glass casket to look at his corpse. The only time they don't let people in there is when they periodically take him out and use formaldehyde to wash down and re-preserve his body. I guess you could say they don't want to wash their dirty Lenin in public! Mohammad is buried in Medina, a city in Saudi Arabia.

I doubt they found a casket big enough for Buddha. However, the body of Buddha lies in a grave in at the bottom of the Himalayan Mountains.

Confucius' tomb, Buddha's tomb, Mohammed's tomb, and Lenin's tomb are all occupied.

But Jesus Christ's tomb is empty! "I [am] he that liveth, and was dead; and, behold, I am alive for evermore, Amen; and have the keys of hell and of death" (Revelation 1:18).

Back in the late 80's, I was given a tape of Dr. S.M. Lockridge preaching about Jesus. It is entitled "That's My King." It is by far the most powerful description of Christ I have ever heard. He starts by saying; "I wish I could describe Him to you. But I can't. He's indescribable, but let me tell you something about Jesus:

> My King was born King. The Bible says He's a Seven
> Way King. He's the King of the Jews—that's a racial King.
> He's the King of Israel—that's a National King. He's the
> King of righteousness. He's the King of the ages. He's the
> King of Heaven. He's the King of glory. He's the King of
> kings and He is the Lord of lords. Now that's my King.

Well, I wonder if you know Him. Do you know him? Don't try to mislead me. Do you know my King?

David said the heavens declare the glory of God, and the firmament shows His handiwork. My King is the only one whom no means of measure can define His limitless love. No far seeing telescope can bring into visibility the coastline of His shore of supplies. No barriers can hinder Him from pouring out His blessing.

Well, well, He's enduringly strong. He's entirely sincere. He's eternally steadfast. He's immortally graceful. He's imperially powerful. He's impartially merciful. That's my King.

He's God's Son. He's the sinner's Savior. He's the centerpiece of civilization. He stands alone in Himself. He's august. He's unique. He's unparalleled. He's unprecedented. He's supreme. He's pre-eminent.

Well, He's the loftiest idea in literature. He's the highest personality in philosophy. He's the supreme problem in high criticism. He's the fundamental doctrine of proved theology. He's the carnal necessity of spiritual religion. That's my King!

He's the miracle of the age. He's the superlative of everything good that you choose to call Him.

Well, He's the only one able to supply all of our needs simultaneously. He supplies strength for the weak. He's available for the tempted and the tried. He sympathizes and He saves. He's strong God and He guides. He heals the sick. He cleanses the lepers. He forgives sinners. He discharged debtors. He delivers the captives. He defends the feeble. He blesses the young. He serves the unfortunate. He regards the aged. He rewards the diligent and He beautifies the meek. Do you know Him?

THERE WAS ONLY ONE PERFECT MAN WHO EVER LIVED THE REST OF US HAVE TO SWIM

Well, my King is the key of knowledge. He's the wellspring of wisdom. He's the doorway of deliverance. He's the pathway of peace. He's the roadway of righteousness. He's the highway of holiness. He's the gateway of glory. He's the master of the mighty. He's the captain of the conquerors. He's the head of the heroes. He's the leader of the legislatures. He's the overseer of the overcomers. He's the governor of governors. He's the prince of princes. He's the King of kings and He's the Lord of lords. That's my King!

His office is manifold. His promise is sure. His light is matchless. His goodness is limitless. His mercy is everlasting. His love never changes. His Word is enough. His grace is sufficient. His reign is righteous. His yoke is easy and His burden is light.

Well. I wish I could describe Him to you, but He's indescribable. He's incomprehensible. He's invincible. He's irresistible.

I'm coming to tell you, the heavens of heavens cannot contain Him, let alone a man explain Him. You can't get Him out of your mind. You can't get Him off of your hands. You can't outlive Him and can't live without Him.

Well, Pharisees couldn't stand Him, but they found out they couldn't stop Him. Pilate couldn't find any fault in Him. The witnesses couldn't get their testimonies to agree. Herod couldn't kill Him. Death couldn't handle Him and the grave couldn't hold Him. That's my King!

He always has been and He always will be. I'm talking about He had no predecessor and He'll have no successor. There was nobody before Him and there'll be nobody after Him. You can't impeach Him and He's not going to resign. That's my King! That's my King!

Thine is the kingdom and the power and the glory. Well, all the power belongs to my King. We're around here talking about black power and white power and green power, but it's God's power. Thine is the power. Yeah. And the glory.

We try to get prestige and honor and glory for ourselves, but the glory is all His. Yes. Thine is the Kingdom and the power and glory, forever and ever and ever and ever. How long is that? And ever and ever and ever and ever. And when you get through with all of the evers, then, Amen!"

Now that is the Jesus I am talking about! There has never been nor will there ever be a man like Jesus. He is everything He said He was, and He is more, so much more. More than your diminutive, finite mind could comprehend if you lived ten trillion life times. To fully understand the fullness of Christ and His incredible grace is impossible. Our capacity to take it all in is infinitely too small. In comparison it would be like trying to fill a ballpoint pen with the Pacific and the Atlantic Ocean. The capacity of the pen is too small and so are we. But one day, when we trade this old corruptible body for one like Jesus's body, then our capacity will be expanded. Isaiah said, for the earth shall be full of the knowledge of the LORD, as the waters cover the sea" (Isaiah 11:9). One grand and glorious day we will walk, on water but until then there was only one perfect man who ever lived; and, He could and still can walk on water the rest of us have to swim!